ENTERPRISE:
Doing Business in America

Titles of Related Interest from MENTOR and SIGNET

ENTERPRISE
Doing Business in America

Commentary by Eric Sevareid
with John Case

A MENTOR BOOK
NEW AMERICAN LIBRARY

New York and Scarborough, Ontario

Cover photo: UPI

WGBH would like to acknowledge the special support of the funders
of the ENTERPRISE television series. They include: The Dun &
Bradstreet Corporation; Merrill Lynch, Pierce, Fenner & Smith
Incorporated; Charles E. Culpeper Foundation; The Arthur Vining
Davis Foundations; The William and Mary Greve Foundation; The
George Gund Foundation; Arthur D. Little, Inc.; Learning Corporation
of America.

Videocassettes of ENTERPRISE television programs are available from
the Learning Corporation of America, 1350 Avenue of the Americas,
New York, NY 10019.

Special thanks are due the producers of the original series of
ENTERPRISE television programs at WGBH Boston: executive
producers **Zvie Dor-Ner** and **Paul Solman**, and producers Tom
Friedman, David Grubin, Chris Hegedus, Louise Henry, Austin Hoyt,
Mike Kirk, Jeff Kirsch, John Nathan, D.S. Pennebaker, and Nancy Porter.

Library of Congress Catalog Card Number: 83-63154

For their invaluable assistance in the preparation of this work, the authors wish to thank:

Alexandra Johnson/David Mehegan/Constance Paige

Contents

Introduction

BY TODAY'S STANDARDS, Calvin Coolidge's dictum "The business of America is business" sounds hopelessly narrow-minded. Certainly no modern president would forget to include education, science, the arts, and half a dozen other areas of endeavor in a litany of the nation's concerns. Still, Coolidge may have been more nearly right than we like to admit. This year, roughly two out of three working Americans will be employed in the private, commercial sector of the economy. Business accounts for about 80 percent of the national income. Through taxes and contributions it makes possible most of the other ventures that make up the fabric of our national life.

There's another sense too in which business is important. Virtually all the institutions we ordinarily think of as noncommercial—universities, government agencies, even churches and charities—are in some ways economic entities. Like a giant corporation or a corner store, they must buy what they need, pay their employees, and find the money to cover these expenses. Management, budgeting, marketing, and the other concepts and techniques of business thus play a role in this context too. There are few human institutions, whatever else they may be, that cannot in some way be defined as a business.

For all that, business occupies a curiously ambiguous place in Americans' minds. Those who are directly concerned with the business world hungrily devour the latest news, much as sports fans pore over the latest reports and statistics. Business students, of whom there are a growing number, eagerly tackle Principles of Accounting 101 or Decision Systems 202. But much of this concern for the trees of the business world obscures the forest. Business as an enterprise, as a dramatic human endeavor capable of bringing out both the best and the worst in people, is a world we rarely see. There are few novels and fewer movies about business. On commercial television, as one recent study found, the businessman or woman is typically portrayed as a clown, a crook, or a con artist.

The Public Broadcasting System's television series *Enterprise* is an attempt to fill this void. The programs profile people at work—executives, managers, entrepreneurs, ordinary workers—as they confront the situations that determine how well their business will do. This is not the stuff of conventional drama. There are no life-or-death situations and few cops and robbers. There is little violence and no sex. The stories are, however, no less compelling for this lack. When people with a lot at stake struggle to make a risky venture come out right, it is hard not to find yourself caught up in the outcome.

At the same time, each *Enterprise* program is a sort of case study, a mini-lesson in the principles and strategies that underlie a business's operation. I don't mean to make it sound either dull or academic, for it is neither. But just as a scientist exploring the frontiers of molecular biology is representative of science itself, so Loy Weston, Tom Gentry, and the others profiled on *Enterprise* are representative of business people at work. The problems they face—of risk, of competition, of trying to sell what they have produced—show in a nutshell how business pursues its objectives. Along the way they teach us a little economics, a little history, and a good deal about the way human beings respond to challenge and opportunity.

THIS BOOK, in a sense, picks up where the television series leaves off. A half-hour film is necessarily concise. It sketches the problems its protagonist faces; it provides enough background information to make the story understood. But it can only hint at the complex mosaic of experience, concepts, and strategies that go into every major business decision. The chapters that follow construct this mosaic in all its richness. They spell out a general problem, then tell the story of people in particular situations as they face the problem.

The first three chapters focus on the fundamentals of business itself. One is entrepreneurship. Frequently, the word *entrepreneur* conjures up a legendary figure like John D. Rockefeller or Henry Ford; at the very least it suggests someone who owns and runs a business, like Texas oilman Bill

Brodnax, whom Chapter One profiles. But Brodnax is not the only entrepreneur to be found in this book, and not all of the others are at the head of their own companies. Some are to be found inside larger organizations, developing new products or new markets or new ways of doing things. Others are trying to engineer new competitive strategies. Still others are trying to help a small company get big or a failing firm to turn itself around. The first chapter looks at the kind of person who is willing and able to wrestle with such tasks.

Chapter Two scrutinizes the marketplace, the turf on which entrepreneurs and managers make their decisions and take their chances. In it, a Kentucky horse breeder named Tom Gentry must gamble on whether a beautiful bay filly that he's putting up for auction will bring what Gentry thinks she should. There is, of course, no ironclad formula by which the value of a thoroughbred racehorse can be calculated; there are only a set of potential buyers and a series of bids. Taken together, these determine both how much this horse is worth and whether Tom Gentry will make the profit he seeks. The auction is thus a sort of microcosmic symbol and representation of the market and its principles in general.

Chapter Three is about risk. Like the first two chapters, it treats a subject that crops up in nearly every business story—whenever, it might be said, entrepreneurs take their products to the marketplace. But risk bears scrutiny all by itself, simply because it is the entrepreneur's constant companion, permeating everything else. When the business in question is as small and as new as the catfish farm described in this chapter, risk seems almost like the lead player in the drama.

Next come three chapters on the first tasks a business faces. One, it has to find financing for a venture. Two, it has to develop a product that is needed and that customers will buy. Three, it has to make sure customers actually do buy the product. A business text might call these subjects finance, product development, and marketing. In real life, as we shall see, they are part and parcel of getting an enterprise started or of moving it from one rung to the next on the ladder of growth.

In Chapter Four a man named John Z. DeLorean undertakes the Herculean task of assembling a new automobile company. DeLorean himself is now notorious mainly for his cocaine-related arrest in late 1982, but before that he was known as a flamboyant and highly accomplished businessman. Could he start a new auto firm where everyone else had failed? How he got as far as he did is a case study in creative finance. How he later ran into trouble is a case study in the uncertainties of the marketplace.

In Chapter Five a company that became famous from one line of clothing stakes its reputation and its profit margins on a venture into quite a different line. Everyone knows that Levi Strauss & Company makes jeans and a variety of other casual clothing and that it's a world leader in these products. Shouldn't that be enough? The truth is, no big company can ever afford to sit back and rest on its laurels. Like Levi, firms must confront the problem of product development—of keeping pace with a changing marketplace—over and over.

Neither, of course, can a firm take its product to market and simply hope that someone will buy. Rather, the product has to be sold. In Chapter Six a pair of case studies illustrates how important and how varied the marketer's job can be. In one, the familiar face of Kentucky Fried Chicken's Colonel Sanders turns up in an unfamiliar setting. Loy Weston, head of KFC's operations in Japan, has the task of introducing the fast-food chicken to the Japanese and of making sure that they buy the Colonel's wares rather than those of his competitors. A similar task faces an unlikely pair of entrepreneurs in another unusual setting. Gordon Thomas and Max Morgan-Witts are best-selling writers, authors of, among other works, a history of the 1929 crash called *The Day the Bubble Burst*. How can readers be persuaded to buy this book? As it turns out, the two are accomplished marketers as well as successful writers. Like Weston, they illustrate how a business goes about selling its wares.

The subsequent three chapters discuss the chief problems entrepreneurs and managers must face in making a success of a venture once it's off the ground. One of course is competition. No business, however big, can ignore the fact that other enterprises would be glad to take away its markets, its customers, or its sources of capital. Sometimes, as the stories of Boeing and Eastern Airlines in Chapter Seven indicate, competition can threaten a company's very existence. At that point the decisions taken by the people at the top suddenly become critical, with millions of dollars and thousands of jobs hanging in the balance.

A second problem is making an organization work. The textbooks might call this subject labor relations or human resource management. Whatever it is called, it is a story of people and how they work together. A business brings together people who must play a variety of roles and who have a variety of interests, yet who all must cooperate to ensure the enterprise's success. A company's approach to this problem reflects culture, history, and managerial style. Chapter Eight's story of a Japanese firm in the United States—Kyocera, based in San Diego—shows how different these all can be.

A business also has to face the possibility of failure. Failure lurks behind all the tasks treated in this book, for at any point an enterprise can find itself without sufficient capital, without a successful product, or without the ability to meet the competition. If enough of these grim possibilities happen at once, a company may face bankruptcy. What does it mean when a firm has to shut up shop? The answer, as the case study in Chapter Nine shows, may be quite surprising: an enterprise that was unsuccessful in one guise may be quite useful to someone else.

The last chapter explores business's role in society. This role has changed considerably over the years—a change illustrated by the unusual history of the American Telephone and Telegraph Company. Can an enterprise serve society's interests as well as its own? I have added an epilogue that discusses different aspects of the same subject. Neither the last chapter nor the epilogue, I fear, will satisfy ideologues of either the right or the left, who have their own preconceived notions about the virtue or iniquity of business. My own goal is modest enough: to explore the conflicting pressures a business faces and the many purposes it may serve. If this sheds some light on an appropriate role for business enterprise in American society, so much the better.

LIKE THE PROTAGONISTS, you the reader will not always anticipate the outcome of the various case studies or the solutions to the problems they present. You will know that you're going to learn something about how business people confront the critical moments and problems in their ventures' lives. And you will learn how they go about making the decisions that eventually determine success or failure.

That, in turn, may help us all understand a little more about our nation's business.

—Eric Sevareid

1. The Entrepreneur

IN 1859 A man named Edwin Drake drilled the first successful oil well. The place was Titusville, Pennsylvania, near a stream known as Oil Creek because of the black film that covered the water.

Oil was already known as a cheap, effective fuel for lighting, and Drake's discovery touched off a rush of prospectors to the area. Soon Titusville and its environs became a "landscape dominated by oil," as the writers Peter Collier and David Horowitz describe it. "Wildcat fires burned day and night; smoke billowed up from engines straining to pump out the precious fluid; oil mixed with mud to form a sticky ooze clinging to horses' legs and wagon wheels and making the roads nearly impassable."

In Cleveland, not long before, John D. Rockefeller and a partner named Maurice Clark had started a commission merchant business, trading in grain and other commodities. By 1863 the business was doing well, thanks partly to wartime orders. So when a friend of Clark's named Samuel Andrews proposed that the partners go into the refining business, Rockefeller was willing to put up $4,000 he had saved. "But he made it clear," Collier and Horowitz note, "that for him the oil venture was subsidiary to the grain business, which had proved itself time and again in recent years as a reliable, if not spectacular, enterprise."

Slowly Rockefeller came to devote more attention to oil and less to grain. In 1865 he bought out Clark for $72,500 and set about expanding the new firm of Rockefeller and Andrews. Soon the company was the largest oil refiner in Cleveland, turning out 500 barrels a day. Its revenues, $1 million in 1865, doubled in 1866. About this time a bystander happened by and caught a glimpse of Rockefeller, who thought himself alone in his office. As the bystander watched —so runs the story—Rockefeller jumped in the air and clicked his heels together, repeating to himself, "I'm bound to be rich! Bound to be rich! *Bound to be rich!*"

The rest, as they say, is history. Rockefeller expanded his refining capacity and leased all the tank cars the railroads had. That left his competitors no way to get their oil out of Cleveland. In 1870, shortly after he had formed the Standard Oil Company, he made a deal with the railroads by which they would charge oil refiners high rates for their shipments but kick back some of the money to Rockefeller and other refiners who were in on the scheme. "Within three months," says one history of the company, "Rockefeller bought up all but 3 of his 25 competitors in Cleveland." Though Standard Oil then controlled a quarter of the nation's refining capacity,

Rockefeller aimed higher. He convinced refiners else-where to join the Standard combine, and "he did it with such secrecy that almost no one knew about his oil monopoly until it was a *fait accompli*. By 1880 Rockefeller was refining 95% of the nation's oil."

In 1906 the Justice Department in Theodore Roosevelt's administration brought suit against Standard Oil under the Sherman Antitrust Act. In 1911 the Supreme Court determined that Standard was indeed a monopoly in violation of the law and ordered it to be broken up into thirty-four separate companies. These firms included Standard Oil of New York, later to become Mobil; Standard of New Jersey, later to become Esso and then Exxon; Standard of California (Chevron); and Standard of Indiana (Amoco). These are among the biggest oil companies operating in the world today. Exxon, the largest, had over $100 billion in sales in both 1980 and 1981—"the first twelve-digit revenue collector," as *Fortune* put it. Ever since Rockefeller the oil business has been dominated by these giants, most notably by his own corporate descendants.

About fifteen years ago, however, the industry began to undergo a slow but massive change. Back then, gasoline sold for perhaps $.35 a gallon, tax included. Home heating oil cost around $.20 a gallon. A barrel of crude oil on the world market went for less than $3.00. America's oil producers, most of them in Texas, still enjoyed a source of wealth—"black gold"—that had by then become legendary. But the marketplace constantly threatened to under-cut them. Oil from the Middle East was cheaper and often lower in sulfur than the domestic variety, and only a limitation on oil imports imposed in the late

1950s ensured that American producers didn't lose all their customers. For decades, too, the threat of overproduction and consequently falling prices plagued Texas oilmen. Only a system of production limits overseen by the Texas Railroad Commission, together with the import quotas, kept domestic prices up. Meanwhile, as the financial writer Adam Smith notes in his book *Paper Money*, the giant oil firms "were trying to think up more ways to sell petroleum products, to burn off what *Fortune* had called the Glut Without End."

For most Americans, the Glut Without End came to an abrupt one in late 1973. Israel and Egypt were at war, and the Arab members of the then-obscure group known as the Organization of Petroleum Exporting Countries (OPEC) announced an embargo on oil shipments to the United States. In December of that year OPEC made a further announcement: henceforth the price of crude oil would be $11.65 a barrel, not $2.70. Before long, cars were backed up at gasoline stations, and the price of petroleum products took off. By 1980, as every driver knew, gasoline was going for between $1.25 and $1.50 a gallon. Only a surplus of petroleum on the world market in late 1981 and 1982 slowed the increase.

Behind the OPEC announcements and price increases was a fundamental shift in the economics of oil. In the ten years from 1960 to 1970, the consumption of oil in the United States rose from 9.8 million barrels a day to 14.7 million. In those years, the economy was thriving. People were buying big cars and driving them on the new Interstate Highway System. (In 1968 the United States had one car for every 2.2 people, as compared with one for every 4 or 5 people in Western Europe and one for every 8 in Japan.) More and more oil was used in home heating, in the production of electricity, and in petrochemical products ranging from paint thinner to Baggies. By 1970 the United States was actually using slightly more energy per dollar of gross national product than it had in 1960—and two or three times as much as other industrial nations used.

Domestic oil production couldn't keep up with this demand. By the early 1970s the wells in Texas and elsewhere were producing at full capacity, something they had never been allowed to do before. By 1973, the year of the embargo, the United States was importing about 38 percent of its oil, as compared with 15 percent in 1959 and 20 percent in 1960. With demand so high and domestic production lagging, some sort of price hike, it is now thought, was inevitable. OPEC merely hastened the process along.

With prices up and existing wells operating at capacity, the seven major oil companies stepped up the pace of their exploration efforts. They couldn't cover the territory, however. Besides, they didn't need to. All the big firms were, and are, vertically integrated companies, with income from refining and marketing oil and petroleum products as well as from exploration and production. All had sources of crude around the world. When OPEC raised its prices, the majors weren't happy about it, but they complained all the way to the bank. Meanwhile, most had started on the road to becoming conglomerates, with a variety of investments outside of oil.

The oil business, it soon became apparent, was a good place for new enterprise. The big firms weren't likely to find all the "grease" that could profitably be produced. But they would be more than happy to buy it, refine it, and sell it, at OPEC-inflated prices. A prospector capable of finding oil could therefore expect to make a killing, at minimal trouble and expense.

Just as it had been in John D. Rockefeller's time, the business was ripe for the peculiar talents of that quintessentially American character, the entrepreneur.

ENTREPRENEURS, in this country, are the stuff of legend. George Eastman invents dry photographic film and a camera to go with it, then creates a company that has dominated the world photographic industry ever since. Henry Ford borrows the idea of an assembly line from Ransom Olds; his new factory can makes cars so much quicker and more cheaply than his competitors that his name becomes synonymous with an inexpensive, practical car. Entrepreneurs whose names are not household words are nonetheless revered in business circles. Alfred P. Sloan, the businessman who built the General Motors colossus, finally saw his company surpass Henry Ford's not so much on the basis of production as on the basis of marketing. (Sloan's idea was to offer customers a different car for every income level, as opposed to Ford's strategy of concentrating on a single basic model.) Thomas Watson, the onetime Ohio farmboy who was fired by National Cash Register in 1913, took a firm called Computer-Tabulating-Recording Company and before his death made it into one of the nation's biggest concerns. Its name now is IBM.

Most entrepreneurship, of course, is considerably less glamorous than these legendary figures would suggest. The owner of a neighborhood dry-cleaning establishment is one sort of entrepreneur. So too are the farmer, the lawyer in solo practice, the engineer who starts a tiny manufacturing firm, and the local plumber. At last count there were nearly 12 million businesses in America run as sole proprietorships, and another million or so run as partnerships. These, plus some fraction of the nation's 2 million corporations, are run by entrepreneurs.

Neither the glamour of legend nor the everyday reality of small business, however, does justice to the role played in our society by the entrepreneur. The economy is not, after all, a placid landscape of giant corporations and corner grocery stores, all of them going about their business in peaceful co-existence. Rather it is a swirling maelstrom of change. Companies are born and die virtually every day. Small firms grow large, sometimes by knocking off a giant. Big firms fight to maintain their competitive position. Every enterprise must take risks, innovate, sell, find money, manage its workers, take on the competition. "Look at the pages of any business journal announcing the ceaseless flow of new products, or at least new wrinkles on old products," suggests the economist Robert Heilbroner; "watch the financial pages for news of mergers or proposed mergers, each seeking to carve out a little protected space in the competitive field; examine the antics of television advertising, giant companies standing on their hands to win customers; peruse the want ads and keep track of strikes—and you will see the market system at work, capitalism thrusting and pulling and pushing itself along, simultaneously building its mighty and its trivial accomplishments while causing its petty and its tremendous disruptions." This dynamic struggle is in many ways the essence of the free-market economy and the origin of the tremendous drama of business.

Entrepreneurs are the lead players in the drama, making their appearance wherever change is in the offing and pushing the change along with their activities. In at least four specific settings their role is crucial. A new industry, first, is typically made possible by technological progress. Just as typically, it depends on entrepreneurs for its growth. Rockefeller didn't discover oil, nor did he invent the internal-combustion engine or any other device utilizing petroleum. But the early growth of the oil business depended more on his efforts than on any other individual's. Similarly, the computer business— today's burgeoning new industry—has depended on the hundreds of engineers and business people willing to take the risks involved with launching a new venture. Not all these ventures, it should be noted, are independent companies. A man like Tom West, the engineer who is portrayed in Tracy Kidder's book *The Soul of a New Machine* as the driving force behind Data General's latest minicomputer, is just as much an entrepreneur as if he had started his own company.

Entrepreneurs are equally important when it comes to launching a new product in an existing industry. No business, however well established and mature, sits still for long. The popular Jordache line of clothing, for example, was started only a few years ago by three brothers who engineered an aggressive new marketing style that brought their company explosive growth. Freddie Laker's cut-rate flights between the United States and Europe a few years ago created, in effect, a new product in the airline industry, the no-frills trip. George Steinbrenner, the free-spending owner of the New York Yankees, created a dynamic new team by taking advantage of a change in major-league baseball's rules governing how, and to whom, a player could sell his services. With the advent of a free agency, as the new system is known, established players could offer themselves on the open market. Steinbrenner's million-dollar salaries made it possible for the Yankees to acquire enough superstars to win several pennants.

Third, the entrepreneur is frequently the one who opens up new markets. Thomas Bata grew up in Czechoslovakia, where his father ran a shoe company. In 1932 the father was killed in a plane crash, and shortly thereafter it became apparent that Czechoslovakia might fall to Hitler. Bata fled his native land, smuggling out bars of gold and shoemaking machinery, and set up shop in Ontario. Today, nearly fifty years later, his subsidiaries are in every part of the globe. The Bata Shoe Company sells some 250 million pairs a year, or roughly one out of every three sold in the noncommunist world. Tom Bata's philosophy, it is said, is summed up in a story he is fond of telling about the two shoe salesmen who were sent to a poverty-stricken country. One wired back, "Returning home immediately. No one wears shoes here." The other cabled, "Unlimited possibilities. Millions still without shoes." In espousing the latter view, Bata typifies the entrepreneurial role.

In addition, the entrepreneur is important when, so to speak, the economic ground shifts. The deregulation of the airlines, as a later chapter will recount, made possible the growth of feisty new carriers capable of challenging the entrenched lines. Trucking deregulation had the same effect. In communications a combination of changing regulations and new technologies has opened up a raft of business possibilities. Television can now be carried by direct-broadcast satellite and by cable and can be made available in videocassette or videodisc forms. A plethora of new companies have entered the telecommunications field, only to find themselves faced with intense competition from new, entrepreneurial divisions of well-established firms. The sea change that characterized the energy industry in the last ten years made it possible, as we shall see, for hustling newcomers to carve out a piece of the action for themselves.

The entrepreneur who takes on all these tasks need not be an "entrepreneur" in the conventional sense, that is, a man or woman who starts and runs a business. Some, as the foregoing examples suggest, take a small company and try to make it big, or take a big one and try to make it do new things and work in new ways or areas. The category of entrepreneur includes all the people who set out to change the corner of the business world in which they find themselves—all the people, in a word, who push the system along its restless path. Only a few wind up as legends. But as a group entrepreneurs are an interesting lot.

Among the most interesting of all entrepreneurs are those who have helped reshape the oil business— the independent prospectors or as they are usually called, wildcatters. One such wildcatter, a burly Texan named Bill Brodnax, illustrates what the entrepreneur does and just how challenging his job can be.

* * *

IN 1965 Bill Brodnax went to work for Humble Oil, now Exxon. It was a good job, and he was good at it. But these were the years when the industry was changing most rapidly. In 1974 Brodnax saw his opportunity. He left Exxon to go out on his own. The company he started was called Taurus Petroleum.

For six years Taurus limped along on the proceeds of an early discovery. Brodnax could probably have been earning a six-figure salary with Exxon; instead he drew little more than expenses from Taurus, plowing most of the money back into new ventures. In 1980 he thought he had a chance at a big strike—a barn-burner. If he was right, he would be a rich man virtually overnight. Better yet, the strike would put Taurus on the map, marking it as an energy-exploration company to be watched. That in turn would mean more and bigger opportunities in the future.

Brodnax's idea, ironically, involved not oil but gas—a 13,500-foot-deep gas well near Lafayette, Louisiana, to be drilled into a geological formation known as the Marg Tex sands. Though the oil business made most of the headlines in the 1970s, the natural gas business wasn't far behind. Gas is often found in conjunction with oil deposits and in fact for many years was simply burned up—flared off—on the spot. But as the price of oil went up, so too did the price of gas. Prospectors like Brodnax found themselves in the energy business, searching for gas, oil, or both.

Two years earlier Exchange Oil and Gas of New Orleans had sunk a successful well only a mile away from Brodanx's proposed site. That well pumped 6 billion cubic feet of gas, worth some $80 million. Other wells drilled later in the same area had come up dry. But the data produced by geologist Keith Barousse, the number-two man in Taurus's four-person operation, had convinced Brodnax that a well on this site could hit the gas field Exchange had discovered. The trick, he thought, was to drill deeper than the others had gone.

Putting together a new venture, however, is never a simple operation. The entrepreneur has to be part hustler and part dreamer, part hard-nosed manager and part charismatic leader. He has to come up with a plan and convince potential backers it is sound. He has to put the money to work effectively, assembling the various pieces into a whole and inspiring both employees and partners to cooperate. All the while he has to plan his next step if the venture succeeds and figure out what to do if it fails.

For Brodnax, as for most entrepreneurs, the first problem was money. The gas well would cost over a million dollars to drill, and Taurus couldn't come close to financing it alone. Nor could the firm depend on conventional sources of finance. No bank, for instance, would lend it money for a well; the chance of a "dry hole" was simply too great. Nor could shares of stock be sold publicly. A stock offering ordinarily requires that a company have a well-defined product, an established market, and a solid track record in business. Occasionally, of course, investors will jump at the chance to buy stock even when these conditions aren't met, as the recent hot offerings of fledgling genetic technology companies indicate. But though the oil and gas a wildcatter may find are easily marketable and potentially profitable, no one knows whether any given wildcatter will find any energy at all, let alone how much and when. Risks of that sort don't usually make for successful stock issues. And from Brodnax's point of view, a public stock offering would mean relinquishing his sole ownership and control of the company.

He did, however, have one asset that most companies do not. He could offer investors a piece of the action in a single venture undertaken by his company, a royalty interest in the gas produced by just this one well. That kind of deal wouldn't involve any repayment if the well came up dry. Nor would it dilute Brodnax's control of Taurus itself. And for the investors, it would mean the chance of a fat payoff in cash in a relatively short period of time.

BEFORE ACTUALLY seeking the money, Brodnax needed to secure drilling rights to the 1,400-acre parcel of land around the proposed site. More than a year before drilling began, he sent landman Pee Wee Whiting to talk to the property owners whose land overlay the reservoir. Whiting's job didn't take long. The twenty-two landowners, many of them farmers, settled for $100 an acre for the first year, $75 an acre therafter if the lease was renwed, and, most important, a one-sixth royalty. The royalty, if the drill struck gas, would bring them nearly 17 cents on every dollar's worth produced. For a typical landowner, the total could be as much as $8,000 a month.

Then came the big job. "Once you own the prospect totally," Brodnax explains, "the next step is to go out and find investors who have drilling bucks, big drilling dollars, who will believe in your geological idea and go along with you." Brodnax's first call was to Marline, a New York-based fund for big investors. Woody Gray of Marline knew Brodnax and didn't need to be convinced. Better, he put Taurus in touch with a company called Energy Sources, Incorporated, a Dallas fund for investors in the $5000 to $10,000 range. Gray also introduced the Taurus group to Walter Worbey of Emerald Oil, a millionaires' fund based in Alberta. Finally, Keith Barousse went on his own to Aminoil in Houston. "He showed them the deal, got them interested," says Brodnax. "They came over and looked at it, and they bought the rest." The final scorecard: Marline would get 25 percent of the revenue from any gas the well produced. Energy Sources and Emerald would each get 15 percent, and Aminoil would get 20 percent. For putting the deal together, Taurus would get a free ride and 25 percent of the net. All told, the deal produced $1.4 million.

For the investors the odds weren't particularly good. Not only do four out of every five wildcat wells drilled in the United States turn up dry, but only one in fifty produces a big strike. Nevertheless, the prospect of a payoff was sufficient to make even these odds pale. The well cost $1.4 million. A big find, Brodnax estimated, could be worth as much as $150 million. Even a decent-sized strike would make it more than worth the investors' while. Walter Worbey of Emerald Oil, for example, could realize a profit of between $3 million and $5 million. Brodnax himself stood to make maybe $30,000 a month for the life of the well.

The drilling funds and other capital sources that wildcatters like Brodnax use take a big risk in putting up their money, but they spread their risks. For one thing, each fund is itself a pool of money from many different individuals—and does not, presumably, include all the money that any one individual has to invest. So even a total loss would mean just one negative factor in that individual's portfolio. For another, the funds invest in a lot of wells: Aminoil, for instance, put up money for over one hundred different ventures the same year it invested in Brodnax. The chance that an individual well will turn up dry may be great, but the overall odds of energy exploration are reasonable.

The funds' decisions about whether to risk money on an individual venture are part rational calculation. Before Aminoil joined the deal, for instance, it went over Taurus's geological maps and projections in detail, satisfying itself that the fundamental idea was sound. But once the calculations were made, some intangibles had to be added in: a blend of hope, faith, intuition, maybe even a certain lack of realism. "When you're evaluating plays," said Dave Ewing, manager of Energy Sources, "it's a funny thing, but you have a gut feeling from the beginning on a play that's good."

And that, for Brodnax, might be the ultimate payoff. If this well hit it big, investors would be his for the asking in the future. "If this one hits, and hits like we think it will," he said, "we'll have a whole lot of gas, a whole lot of money, and we will have been able to prove to a group of people who invested their money with us that we knew what we're doing. They're going to stay with us, and that's going to allow us to drill a lot more wells with this same bunch of people."

COMPANIES LIKE Brodnax's Taurus Petroleum have come to play an increasingly important role in the industry. Taurus is one of 12,000 independent producers looking for oil and gas in the United States; collectively they drill more than 60,000 wells a year, or more than 90 percent of the national total. Though many wells turn up dry, the independents as a group have a good record. Their funds account for half of all new producing oil wells and nearly three-quarters of all new gas wells. Recently many have run into trouble as energy prices have leveled off and demand slackened. But the longer-term prospects are still bright. As Will Rogers said in his advice to buy land, "they ain't makin' any more of the stuff." The same is true of oil and gas.

With the investors on board, Brodnax hires the rig: the raising of the derrick marks the end of eighteen months of planning and the beginning of several weeks of drilling. Now there are other kinds of obstacles. Drilling into high-pressure sands, for example, can blow the well out. Forty miles away, a Chevron well blew out, and the escaping gas caught fire. It took a week to cap that one. Here at Taurus's rig—it's called Glasscock No. 64—the drillers are worried. They can counter the high pressure with a heavy drilling fluid called mud. But to know what weight of mud to circulate down the hole, they have to know exactly where they are. Right now, they don't. Even more difficult, part of the hole has to be lined with steel casing, because of the pressure. Taurus has two miles of the casing waiting to be set, but for that too the drillers need to know how deep the hole is.

With drilling nearing the critical high-pressure depth, a paleontologist named Ray Bane is called in. If he can find "bugs"—fossils of microscopic organisms—of the sort found in the dry well drilled nearby, he'll know how deep the Taurus drill has gone. Finally, at 2:00 A.M., Bane finds what he's looking for. At 10,900 feet the drilling stops, and the workers begin to set the protective casing. Mud weighing up to seventeen pounds per gallon circulates through this casing, providing enough weight to hold back the pressure below.

At last it's seventy-two feet to TD—total depth. Drilling superintendent Bill Tilley calls Brodnax and tells him drilling will take only six more hours, plus another five hours to pull out of the hole. Brodnax calls the investors. After awhile he asks Tilley if there are any signs of gas: there are none. But the results, Brodnax knows, aren't final. "You sit here and bite buttonholes in your seat until you get that log on the ground and then you can look at it," he explains. "It doesn't make a hill of beans what you think or what you predict or anything else. So we'll just sit here and sweat until 6:00 A.M. and see what we got."

That night there's a party at the Rim Rock Lounge, a favorite haunt of the Lafayette oil crowd. One by one the investors begin to show up. So too does their nervousness. "The deal looks as good or better than it was presented to us on paper," says Emerald's Walter Worbey. "But that definitely does not guarantee we've got a well."

Next morning, the logging instruments get the results, and Keith Barousse brings them in. They are plain as day, no doubt about them. A dry hole. "Read it," says Brodnax, "and weep."

No one in the wildcatting business, however, will weep for too long. "We're going to be drilling some more," said Worbey when the news was announced. "Not tomorrow, but in a week or so, we'll feel better and start all over again." Brodnax agreed. "Tomorrow you start thinking about where you're going to drill the next well. Forget this one. Get some more bits turning to the right. Can't find oil sitting on your butt."

In the end the results for the year weren't so bad. Walter Worbey's Calgary millionaires roughly broke even, with one oil discovery and four dry holes. The high rollers in Marline did better, with 21 producers and 20 dry holes; the payoff was close to three to one. Energy Sources' low rollers turned up eight producers and seven holes, paying roughly two to one. Aminoil found 44 discoveries out of 101 wildcat wells, well above the industry average. Bill Brodnax started the year $300,000 in debt from the purchase of new leases. In six months he drilled four small oil wells, all producers. "An oilman is never poor while he's alive," says Bob Edge, another Texas wildcatter. "He's just broke from time to time."

WHAT MAKES ENTREPRENEURS like Brodnax tick? Part of the answer, obviously, is money. A strike on the Marg Tex, or any other barn-burner, would mean hundreds of thousands of dollars, more than Brodnax could earn in several years of corporate employment. In general the entrepreneur taps a unique source of wealth. Doctors, lawyers, and consultants may be very well paid, but ordinarily their earnings are linked to the time that they as individuals can work. The man or woman who starts a business is creating an entity whose worth has only to do with how much money it can generate, not with how much time is put into it. Suppose, for example, that an entrepreneur starts a business that represents an investment of $1 million and turns a profit of $200,000. Already his or her income will be well beyond what all but the very highest paid professionals can expect to earn. If, moreover, the prospect is for further growth, the $1-million real investment may be worth considerably more than that to a prospective purchaser. This phenomenon can be seen when a new computer firm, for instance, "goes public," selling its stock on the open market. Investors may be eager to buy shares, in hopes that the firm will grow rapidly, and bid the price up. Those who started the firm—and who, presumably, bought shares for a nominal cash investment—realize what the economist Lester Thurow has termed "instant wealth."

Just as obviously, however, money isn't everything. If it were, the successful entrepreneur's career would probably be relatively short. The business, after all, can be sold, and the entrepreneur can retire comfortably on the proceeds. Even corporate entrepreneurs, paid handsome salaries and rewarded with bonuses and stock options, could easily give up enterprise for golf after ten years at the top. "Once you are wealthy, you are financially independent, [and] that objective is accomplished," one entrepreneur told Joshua Ronen, a New York University professor who has studied entrepreneurship. "It must be something in addition to that."

There are, to be sure, other easily recognized rewards that come from successful entrepreneurship. Prestige is one. Power, at least over one's own organization, is another. The satisfaction of being in charge is a third. Perhaps less widely recognized is the gambler's instinct. Nelson Bunker Hunt, son of the late oil magnate H. L. Hunt, captured this spirit not long ago with what may rank as the financial understatement of the year. By manipulating his silver holdings in an attempt to corner the market, Hunt had wreaked havoc on that market itself, threatening the stability of the brokerage houses and exchanges involved in the trading of silver. When asked what he thought of his part in silver's price upheavals and their effects, Hunt replied, "It was a game."

Possibly the most fundamental explanation of the entrepreneurial drive is the simple human drive to accomplishment, to do a challenging job well and leave one's mark on the world. Business in this respect is a unique field of endeavor. Unlike sports or the arts, it seems to demand no exceptional innate talent. Unlike science or medicine, it doesn't necessarily require extensive education. And unlike a politician, the entrepreneur does not need to find satisfaction in being a public figure. The opportunities afforded by business, moreover, are varied. People uncomfortable with a large business can start a small one; people unhappy with Wichita can move to San Diego. There is no single center of action, and there is no single track to success.

Then too, failure does not mean the end of one's career. A Texas entreprenuer named Charles Tandy knew both success and failure. Inheriting his family's business, a small Fort Worth leather store, he turned it into a nationwide chain. But when he tried to branch out beyond leather goods, nothing seemed to work. Oil wildcatting, real estate, even a venture into a Texas department store didn't pay off. Finally he bought a Boston-based chain of electronics outlets, itself failing, named Radio Shack. Today Tandy/Radio Shack is a billion-dollar corporation at the top of the market in home electronics. Similarly, a Hungarian-born physicist named Zoltan J. Kiss started a company in 1969 that was one of the earliest producers of liquid crystal display technology. In 1976 the company was forced into bankruptcy. By 1982, however, Kiss was at the head of another company, a leader in the new field of photovoltaics, or sun-generated electricity. Merrill Lynch analysts, hired by the new company to run its marketing and capital-raising operations, told *The New York Times* that Kiss had "as much as a two-year lead over the competition."

One of Joshua Ronen's entrepreneurs probably sums up the entrepreneurial motivation best: "I think the primary objective of an entrepreneur is to create, to develop something new, to push back frontiers and to see that creation resolved in some commercial . . . application." Nowhere can this motivation be seen so clearly as in the case of "repeat" entrepreneurs—those who leave a successfully operating company that they started in order to try starting another one. William Poduska, for instance, made a name for himself in electronics when he founded Prime Computer, a fast-growing concern based near Boston. In 1980 Poduska started another firm, Apollo Computers, specializing in high-performance microcomputers for use by scientists and engineers. Two years later Apollo was claiming sales of $15 million a year and a market valuation of nearly $100 million.

In one sense the entrepreneur is a product of the system, a person who takes advantage of the opportunities provided by a dynamic economy. Poduska found himself in a fast-growing industry; Brodnax found himself in one that was changing dramatically. In another sense, though, the system depends on the entrepreneur. Without the talents, drive, and accomplishments of people who set out to change things, the economy would stagnate. In a world where energy is costly and competition acute, no country can afford stagnation.

From their own perspective, entrepreneurs have a difficult enough task. They have to build up new industries, new products, and new markets; scare up money; motivate people; sell the goods; worry about the competition. From society's perspective, they have an even more difficult job. They, more than anyone else, have to keep the economy moving and changing. A century ago the business genius of John D. Rockefeller created an institution capable of putting petroleum into the hands of consumers throughout the United States. A decade ago it seemed as if the petroleum was finally beginning to run out. Now no one is quite sure what the future holds. There may be more energy to be found in the ground. and there may be other ways of producing power that we have not yet perfected.

But though the outcome is in doubt, the process, it is safe to say, will depend on people like Brodnax, entrepreneurs who are willing to take risks and able to keep on doing so until they succeed.

THE STORY of business inevitably begins with entrepreneurs. They are the people who make things happen. But the world of business turns on considerably more than individual initiative. It demands a social environment—laws, customs, and institutions—that enables people to buy and sell freely.

That environment is the market economy, in everyday parlance the marketplace. Like democracy, equality, and other revolutionary notions, the free market is a child of the eighteenth century. Philosophically it came of age in 1776, with the publication of Adam Smith's *The Wealth of Nations*. A hundred years later it was the central organizing principle of economic life in the industrial world.

The market makes business possible. But it plays another role too: economic judge and jury. In this guise it can be a harsh mistress, determining which businesses will survive and which will die. Success in the marketplace depends not solely on hard work and enterprise, but on whether the market judges your wares to be worth enough for you to stay in business. The price is right, after all, only when buyers are buying and sellers are making money.

Chapter Two tells the story of a man whose success or failure hinged, for the moment at least, on the market's decision about what he was selling. The story says much about how a product's value is determined—and how uncertain life can be for an entrepreneur in the market.

—Eric Sevareid

2. The Marketplace

"KIREI NA IRO. Beautiful color." The voice verges on the shout that Americans habitually employ when speaking to foreigners. The listener, a Japanese investor, blinks in disbelief, fixing his stare on the fiery apparition before him. The speaker is a forty-four-year-old Southerner, with glasses tinted just a shade cooler than the red that inflames his hair, flushes his face, and spills out the top of his white polo shirt. Below the shirt is still more color, a pied madras pair of trousers whose patchwork design seems a gaudy mirror of the surrounding Kentucky countryside.

Kazuo Nakamura, the investor, recognizes those trousers. Two years ago, Nakamura paid a record $1.6 million for a colt owned by Kentucky breeder Tom Gentry, the red-haired man standing before him. Gentry threw a jacket in with the deal, for reasons Nakamura has yet to divine. But there is no mistaking that pattern. Gentry's crazy-quilt trousers are identical to the coat Nakamura got with his thoroughbred racehorse. If nothing else, they mark Gentry as a man not dominated by the dictates of fashion.

Now, standing next to Gentry, is the colt's half-sister, a bay filly. The last offspring of a champion line, she is an investor's dream, and she will go on sale in just three days. Her sire was Hoist the Flag, the fourth-ranked purse winner in American racing and sire of twenty-five stake winners. Her name of the moment, Hoist the Flag filly, lets no one forget the pedigree. Neither do her markings. Like her sire, the filly boasts a distinctive white streak cascading down her forehead like an elegant caste mark. Her coloring, a deep burnished red, shimmers in the morning light. Tom Gentry is right. *Kirei na iro.* Beautiful color.

The question of the moment, though, is not the filly's beauty. On that there is no disagreement. The real issue, for Nakamura and Gentry alike, is both more basic and more contentious. Six months ago Gentry paid a whopping $320,000 for the filly. This weekend he hopes to sell her for a cool half million—a profit of over 50 percent in half a year. Nakamura or somebody else may buy her, but not necessarily at that price. Right now, neither he nor Gentry knows the answer to the question that will be resolved beyond dispute in just a few days.

How much, in dollars, is the Hoist the Flag filly worth?

BUSINESS, a wag has said, consists of capitalist acts between consenting adults. Somebody offers something for sale; somebody else decides to buy it.

In that moment an item's value is suddenly determined. So, too, in a sense, is the future of a business enterprise. If the goods offered for sale can be sold at a profit, the business succeeds. If not, the business fails. The turf on which the entrepreneur wins or loses this gamble is familiar to all, yet elusive in its workings. It is, of course, the marketplace.

Like most modern inventions, the marketplace is taken for granted. Yet it is a historical phenomenon of relatively recent vintage. Indeed, commerce and money have existed since ancient times. But for most of history they played a minor role in most people's lives. Much more important than commercial exchanges were what the economic historian Carlo M. Cipolla calls transfers of income or wealth. Transfers in preindustrial society could take a variety of forms. A peasant might give his landlord a fixed proportion of his crop as rent. A rich man might distribute alms to the poor. Peasant and noble alike might share what they had with the church. And thieves were happy to appropriate wealth to themselves. "As time progressed and civilization developed," writes Cipolla in his book *Before the Industrial Revolution*, "the system slowly changed . . . , but the world in which exchanges are by far the predominant type of transaction emerged only in the last few centuries."

In the preindustrial world, trade and commerce were necessarily quite different from what we think of today. The only merchants many people came into contact with were traveling peddlers gathering at the occasional fair or market day. Most manufacturing was conducted by artisans, sometimes working alone and sometimes with apprentices, but almost never with help that could be regarded as wage labor. What little trade existed was limited, for the most part, to high-quality, costly goods. "Hence," says Cipolla, "the large share of spices and expensive wines in the international exchange of primary products and the large share of luxury cloths in the international exchange of textiles."

Why was commerce so limited? An obvious reason is simply that there wasn't much to trade. The great bulk of nearly everyone's expenditure, rich and poor alike, went for food, clothing, and shelter. And only the rich could afford more than the bare minimum. "In preindustrial Europe," notes Cipolla, "the purchase of a garment or of the cloth for garment remained a luxury the common people could only afford a few times in their lives." By the same token, few could buy the manufactured goods that were available for sale. Since each had to be laboriously crafted by hand, its cost was usually well beyond what all but a noble could pay.

A second obstacle to business was the primitive nature of what economists call an infrastructure. Roads were rough and populated by brigands. Sea travel was perilous. Communication was slow and most of the population illiterate. Most European countries were not nations at all in the modern sense but simply collections of baronies and fiefdoms whose lords may or may not have pledged allegiance to a king. In such a society there was little incentive and little opportunity for even the most enterprising soul to venture beyond the confines of his community. Even if he did, the accouterments of business—an established body of contract law, a universal system of money, a generally understood system of accounting—were in most places only poorly developed.

Finally, the prevailing ideology of feudal society did not allow for much in the way of enterprise. A peasant's duty was to till the land and serve his lord. The lord's duty was to serve the king, seek honor in battle, protect his vassals and serfs. Only the city dwellers escaped this rigorous set of prescriptions—city air, it was said, makes a man free—but for much of the preindustrial period they were few in number. Partly because there was so little room for commerce in the mainstream of European society, what room there was for business endeavors was often filled by Jews—who, as social outcasts, were less governed by conventional rules or expectations.

As CITIES BEGAN to grow and lines of communication and travel opened up, so too did business slowly begin to flourish. The Hanseatic League, most active in the fourteenth century, was a loose federation of traveling merchants, centered in seventy German towns, which controlled nearly all the commerce in the Baltic and North Sea areas. Later the League was supplanted in importance by the Italian sedentary merchants—a term that denotes not their style of life but their fixed locations—and they in turn came to be dominated by the great banking houses such as the Medicis and Fuggers. Finally, in the seventeenth century, the rise of the English and Dutch East India companies—in which members pooled their capital to carry out what amounted to massive economic enterprises involving exploration and colonization—foreshadowed the rise of the modern corporation.

Two other developments made possible the rise of the market economy. One, of course, was the industrial revolution itself, the phenomenal increase in productive power made possible by the use of machines. That made business much more profitable than it had been. The second was the gradual decay of the old social order, in which people's positions and duties were prescribed. As merchants and businessmen grew more powerful, so too did their occupations grow more legitimate and their activities less extraneous to society's central concerns. The "Protestant ethic" identified by Max Weber, in fact, infused the businessman's role with virtue: slowly the possibility of bettering oneself through enterprise came to be seen not only as an opportunity but as a duty. The Calvinist notion of, as Weber describes it, "the necessity of proving one's faith in worldly activity," was only the most extreme version of this marriage of ethics and enterprise.

The classic justification for the marketplace was Adam Smith's *An Inquiry into the Nature and Causes of the Wealth of Nations*, published in 1776. Smith, a Scot, was for many years a professor of moral philosophy. His concern in *The Wealth of Nations*, however, was not so much morality per se as sociology and economics. And his contention was, for the times, startling. People pursuing their own economic self-interest, he said, were working for the good of all. "It is not from the benevolence of the butcher, the brewer or the baker that we expect our dinner but from their regard for their own interest. We address ourselves not to their humanity but to their self-love, and never talk to them of our necessities but of their advantage."

The institution that made it possible for self-interest

to become common interest was the market. Entrepreneurs trying to make a profit would have to provide their customers with the best goods available at the lowest possible price. Should any one of them try to get away with shoddy merchandise or overcharging, a competitor would drive him out of business. Should too many entrepreneurs try to enter the same business, the resulting low prices would make it impossible for the least efficient among them to continue, and they in turn would look for a line of work that was under- rather than over-populated. The businessman, said Smith, "neither intends to promote the public interest, nor knows how much he is promoting it." By running his business "in such a manner as its produce may be of the greatest value, he intends only his own gain, and he is in this, as in many other cases, led by an invisible hand to promote an end which was no part of his intention."

"Thus," says the historian Bruce Mazlish in an introduction to Smith's work, "the gentle, self-effacing selfless Adam Smith transmuted what had traditionally been regarded as evil into good." Thus too did he establish a justification for the role the marketplace was coming to play in regulating economic life. After Smith, free exchange between buyers and sellers was not only a social phenomenon but a social goal, an objective to be pursued through law and policy. As the objective was pursued, the change was dramatic. In the century that followed the publication of Smith's treatise, the market came to be the central organizing principle of economic life in the developed nations. In the noncommunist world it remains so today.

*   *   *

FROM THE ENTREPRENEUR'S or manager's perspective, of course, the market isn't so much a principle as it is a collection of people, all of whose wants and needs must be taken into account. It is the world of customers, both actual and potential, that will ultimately determine how well the business's goods or services sell. It is the suppliers competing with each other to provide materials. It is workers—the "labor market"—willing to do a manager's bidding in return for a given wage. And it is competitors trying to take business away. Rarely does the market seem like an abstract invisible hand that mechanically determines outcomes. On the contrary, it is more like a playing field where business woos its customers and takes on its antagonists.

For Tom Gentry the marketplace of the moment is the Keeneland Summer Select Sale, held every July on a 431-acre complex near Lexington, Kentucky. Keeneland is the Mecca of equine auctions. Unlike Saratoga's Fasig-Tipton sale in August or Florida's Ocala auction in October, Keeneland is restricted to potential stakes winners. Some of the buyers are oil tycoons or celebrities looking for high-stakes gambles. Others are sharp-eyed experts representing well-heeled investment syndicates. The sellers are the thoroughbred horse breeders of bluegrass Kentucky, aristocrats with names like Combs and Hancock and upstarts like Tom Gentry. At Keeneland the sun-drenched greenery and quiet conversation that give the sale its character are deceptive. For despite the genteel trappings, thoroughbreds are a business where fortunes are made and lost. And they are a business that depends more on salesmanship, financial acumen, and managerial skill than most of the old-line breeders would care to admit. Gentry has made them realize that, for he has proved himself a master of the art of raising and selling horses on the marketplace.

Born on the wrong social end of Lexington, Gentry had to earn the world his future rivals would casually inherit. His father, Olin, was one of four Texas brothers who all became leading jockeys; he rode in his first race in Juárez, Mexico, at the age of thirteen, three days before Pancho Villa took over the town. Olin Gentry later migrated to Kentucky. There he began managing Col. E. R. Bradley's Idle Hour Stock Farm, raising scores of racers, including four Kentucky Derby winners.

Tom Gentry grew up on the farm and got his first pony at four, not an unusual event among horse-loving families. His next step was a little more unusual: he bought his first thoroughbred, a Mahmoud named Rancor, at age thirteen, using $3,000 he had saved up. At sixteen he sold his first yearling: the price was $11,000. While a senior at Lexington Catholic High, Gentry was already listed in *Who's Who in Horsedom*, and he was the youngest person ever invited to join the Thoroughbred Club of America. In 1955, a few months after entering the University of Kentucky's School of Agriculture, Gentry made his debut as an agent at Keeneland. By 1959 he ranked as Keeneland's leading agent buyer. Not long after, he bought a mare named First Aid for $4,000 from newspaper tycoon John S. Knight and sold her foal a year later for $29,000. The $25,000 paid for his first breeding farm.

Helped along by monthly boarding fees from wealthy clients like Bing Crosby and Don Ameche, Gentry's operation concentrated on buying high-quality mares and reselling them, then using the profit to upgrade the stock. "Tom started with just a few mares," recalls Tom Hammond, an early partner. "But even then they were all a half-sister or some other relation to a major stakes winner." And he began earning money, not only for himself but for Hammond and many other people. Soon the late A.B. "Bull" Hancock, a legendary Kentucky breeder, began sending his buyers over. When a Gentry colt, Pamir, turned a $240,000 profit for Hancock a year later, buyers like metals magnate Charles Engelhard and oilman Nelson Bunker Hunt flocked to Gentry's sales.

Part of Gentry's success can be traced to hard work. Even now, as in the past, he puts in a twelve-hour day. Up at five-thirty, he turns his seventy-five horses out to pasture by seven, makes the breeding and teasing rounds from nine to twelve and later from four to seven. His routine ensures a kind of quality control, for he insists on supervising every aspect of farm life, from painting fences to planning what color a yearling will be. Years ago he planted hundreds of trees to shade his mares, erected miles of fencing to protect them, and even imported special alfalfa pellets from a nearby Trappist monastery to make their coats shiny. Today a closed-circuit Sony sits on his desk, allowing him to monitor the mares even while he does his ever-growing load of paperwork. "My father taught me to look after everything yourself," he says. "And above all, when it comes to breeding horses, never to pinch pennies."

The other key to Gentry's success is his flair for promotion. When he left Nakamura Saturday morning, he pressed a red ballpoint pen marked with the name TOM GENTRY into the Japanese investor's hand. When he walked over to Barn 17, his headquarters at Keeneland, he passed a bank of outdoor videos showing his colts bounding across the fields. That night, he entertained friends, associates, and potential customers like Nakamura at a lavish banquet, ferrying them over to his farm by helicopter and bringing in Bob Hope to entertain them.

Gentry's flamboyant promotional activities have long been his trademark. In 1969, when 35-degree weather was keeping buyers from his barn at Keeneland's November breeding-stock sale, Gentry set up a free coffee concession flanked by waiters with "cream" and "sugar" stitched on their jackets. Investors flocked to Gentry's barn, but blueblood breeders were so shocked by his social impertinence that, chagrined, he took the stands down. The next day, however, he was vindicated: Keeneland president Louis Lee Haggin told him, "That's the best idea I've heard in years. Put it back." In another well-reported incident, the late Charles Engelhard once paid $7,000 for an inexpensive Gentry yearling despite the fact that Engelhard's purchases were ordinarily in the $30,000 range. "That," he said, "was to pay for all those damn pens and pocket knives I've gotten from Tom over the years."

In this particular auction Gentry has a dozen yearlings up for sale. The prices they bring will determine his profit-and-loss picture for the next twelve months. "Keeneland is a wrap-up of two years' work narrowed down to one or two hours of each evening," he says. "This is the sale that generates enough revenue to make you or break you. Nothing in between." The *pièce de résistance* this year was to be the Hoist the Flag filly. Gentry had bought her six months earlier at Keeneland's six-day January sale. Ordinarily, he says, that is "a sale for leftovers."

But this year former Keeneland president Haggin was putting some of his horses up. Gentry's $32,000 bid for the filly set a record. "It's a rarity to be able to buy into an estate like his," he explained, "and I knew she was worth it."

Two months before the Summer Select, though, the filly developed a problem: an inflammation of her sesamoids, the cartilage around her right front ankle. Sesamoiditis, while not congenitally serious, can indicate a subtle fracture. Ever since May, Gentry and his veterinarian had lavished care on the filly, wrapping her ankles in soft casts to shrink the sesamoids. On July 1 the news wasn't good. "There was a marked improvement," Gentry said, "but the inflammation was still noticeable." Then, twelve days later, the vet announced that the X rays showed no fracture. The filly could make the trip to Keeneland and race with the best of them. Still Gentry's concern did not disappear. Worried that careless buyers might prod and inflame the sesamoids, he knew that mere whisper of the ailment could be fatal to her prospects this weekend.

He had, in fact, a decision to make. Maybe he shouldn't try to sell her this year at all. "How much was it worth for me to tie up my investment for another year and a half?" he asked. Would the price be higher next year? What was she worth to him, or to any potential buyers? This questions plagued him right up to the day of the sale. At that point, of course, her worth would be determined—on the marketplace.

IN A SENSE, determining the price of an item that is up for sale is the market's chief job. Buyer and seller come together, but unless the price is right, no business will be transacted. This, of course, is where the market's law of supply and demand comes in. Theoretically, if buyers want more of something than is readily available, the price will rise. That will cut down on the number of interested buyers and increase the number of interested sellers. If buyers, by contrast, are in short supply, the price will fall. That will make buying look more attractive and selling less so.

The workings of the marketplace in this pure form can be seen most plainly in the stock market. There, anything that makes a company look good to investors will almost immediately drive its stock price up. Reports that a company is failing will cause the price of its stock to plummet. More often, of course, the workings of the market in determining an item's price are neither so quick nor so impersonal. Rather, price is simply one element of the strategy a business pursues as it tries to sell its wares. Automobile companies, for instance, put a "sticker price" on every car they sell. Depending on business conditions, competition, and a host of other considerations, auto dealers may try to get the sticker price for their cars, or they may be willing to give customers deep discounts. A restaurant owner faced with declining business could cut the restaurant's prices just like an auto dealer. More likely, he or she would decide instead to change the menu, fire the chef, or redecorate the dining room. The price of an item thus reflects a complex and lengthy series of calculations in which consumers try to decide how much something is worth to them and businesses try to decide how they can best make money selling it.

Often an item that is high-priced and that therefore seems intrinsically valuable is costly only because of market manipulations. An example of such a process can be found in Edward Jay Epstein's account of what he calls "the diamond invention"— the process by which diamonds were transformed from attractive but essentially useless stones into items of immense value.

Until the late nineteenth century, as Epstein explains it, diamonds were rare and little valued. A huge find near the Orange River in South Africa then swamped the market and threatened to drive the price down even farther. The investors backing the mine realized that their find would be worth little unless the stones were perceived by the public to be both scarce and valuable. Over the years the organization they formed—De Beers Consolidated Mines, Ltd.—accomplished this goal through two methods. It bought up access to or control over virtually all the world's sources of diamonds, thus enabling it to control the gem's supply. At the same time it conducted massive advertising campaigns designed to convince consumers not only that diamonds were desirable—a symbol of love, especially appropriate for engagement rings—but that diamonds were "forever."

The last was important. If consumers, who are estimated to hold some 500 million carats' worth of gem diamonds, ever began to sell their stones off, the price of diamonds would fall quickly. "For the diamond invention to survive," Epstein writes, "the public must be inhibited from ever parting with its diamonds." Jewelers, who have little enough interest in buying stones from customers (they can get them from wholesalers on consignment anyway), also have an interest in maintaining the notion that diamonds are forever. They are thus reluctant to purchase any of the stones they sell back. A diamond ring that is "worth" $2,000 in the jewelry store is thus "worth" only $600 or so when it is sold to one of the few firms that do buy used diamonds.

In principle, the value of a racehorse should be easier to determine than that of a diamond. The horse, after all, is primarily an investment. Its price therefore can be expected to reflect how much money investors think the horse will earn them. In fact, however, the calculations that determine a horse's price are no less idiosyncratic. The reason is simply that horse buying necessarily involves risk. The ways in which an individual investor weighs those risks determine how much he or she is willing to pay.

Keeneland is, to be sure, a regulated market. Of the 900 yearlings nominated for the sale last year, only 300 made the grade. To qualify, a horse must boast an impressive three-generation pedigree, produced by the statistical bureau of the Jockey Club and analyzed by a special four-man committee. If the committee grades the pedigree A, a horse has a good chance of making the auction; a B grade lessens its chances; and a C eliminates them altogether. Nominated yearlings must then pass a confirmation test based on physique and bearing. Several months before the sale, Keeneland veterinarians Dewitt Owne and Arthur Davidson perform the examination, circling each horse front to flank. With so rigorous a screening process, the Keeneland Summer Select effectively sets a floor under its horses' selling prices.

Not even Keeneland, however, can eliminate risk. For one thing, thoroughbreds are notoriously fragile animals, prone both to injuries and to a variety of disorders. Timely Writer, the favorite to win the 1982

Kentucky Derby, for example, had to be scratched just a few days before the race; he had developed severe gastroenteritis and required immediate surgery. But even horses in prime physical shape don't necessarily win races. This year only one out of ten racers will earn the $15,000 necessary to cover its costs. The mating game is equally chancy. A costly broodmare mated to a stallion for a stud fee of $100,000 may produce a foal that is badly formed and therefore unsalable. A stallion rushed too soon to stud may, like Spectacular Bid, initially fail to perform. He can fail his fertility test, or he can turn out to be what's known in the trade as a "shy breeder."

Investors do, of course, have some rules of thumb to go by in determining what they think a horse is worth. Fillies, which are frequently referred to as the cash registers of the market, are thought to be the least risky. A well-bred filly typically produces six live foals. Each yearling ordinarily sells for one-fifth of its mare's market value plus twice the stud fee: for example, a yearling produced by a $50,000 mare mated to a stallion for $10,000 will sell for around $30,000. Since fillies are often bred for pedigree alone, the price of broodmares in the last decade has soared. "A filly always has residual value," Gentry partner Robert Meyerhoff explains. "Even if she never races, her bloodlines are such that she still appreciates in value."

The potential big money—and the potential big bath—lie in colts. And it is colts that dominate the conversation at the Keeneland previews. Will Dance Spell, a Gentry colt up for auction Tuesday, turn out to be the champion runner its owner predicts? If so, his future owners can syndicate him as a stud for princely sums. Syndication is the process by which investors spread the risk, dividing up or selling the forty shares set on each stallion. A share may cost anywhere from $10,000 to $700,000. But since a stallion can service forty mares a year, the stud fees can produce a handsome return. If a colt has a mediocre track record, however, investors may recover as little as 10 percent of their original investment.

Only one factor has nothing to do with racing performance: the tax write-off. For years the government has allowed special tax credits in areas of high-risk investment, and thoroughbreds are among the most attractive, even to investors who wouldn't know a filly from a furlong. An investor who buys a $100,000 prize yearling, for example, can deduct $12,000 a year for the colt or filly's expenses; then, when the horse begins racing at age three, the investor can write off $33,000 a year for any three years during the next six. "If you're an art collector, you can't deduct a bad painting," notes Meyerhoff. "But it's the opposite with horses."

All these considerations—risks, rewards, earnings, liabilities, tax write-offs—enter into the investors' calculations as they consider their bids. The figuring is seldom simple. In the past, what a horse was worth depended on what he could earn, and what he could earn was linked to what was bet. During the last ten years, though, purses at U.S. ractracks rose only 250 percent while yearling prices were soaring 600 percent. The disparity between these figures suggests that more was at work than a simple cost-benefit analysis of the sort one might make in deciding to buy a stock or a bond. Horse racing has always been a glamorous enterprise, for example, tinged with aristocratic overtones. Some investors may have been buying into it partly for the prestige involved. Then, too, the infusion of money from new sources such as wealthy Arabs and Japanese may have helped push prices upward.

Lastly, some of the price rise may have been due to what economists call a bubble phenomenon, in which people buy something simply because they expect prices to continue rising. In the late 1970s, for instance, investors all over the country were scrambling to buy California real estate. These investors didn't necessarily want to live there, nor did they expect that the investment's direct return (in the form of rents from tenants) would necessarily be particularly lucrative. Rather, they expected to make a killing on the continued appreciation of their property, realizing their gains when they sold out. By 1982, of course, the market had softened in California, and investors who had gone deeply into debt to buy property at inflated prices found themselves saddled with high mortgage rates and no chance of selling at a profit. If bubble psychology is at work in the thoroughbred market, prices can be expected to fluctuate dramatically as investors alternately feel optimistic or pessimistic about the market's direction.

The price of a horse, in sum, reflects hard-nosed calculations about what investors can expect to earn on their money and how much risk they are willing to assume in order to earn that return. It also reflects a series of idiosyncratic calculations, such as the wish to be able to tell a friend you own a share of Spectacular Bid. And it reflects an estimation of what the market itself is likely to do in the future. In all these respects, the way the market values a horse is similar to the way it values nearly everything else. Most goods, to be sure, are not investments; they are bought to be used. But the consumer nevertheless weighs judgments about value, about prestige or sex appeal or status, and about what's likely to happen in the future before making a decision to buy. Only when that decision is made, and the price of a product thereby agreed upon, does the item acquire a definite value. Up to then, all it has is an asking price.

As TUESDAY night approaches, Tom Gentry is performing his own set of calculations, designed to determine that asking price. He needs to cover his $1 million yearly overhead, but he must be careful to avoid an unexpectedly high profit. Last year's $2.8 million profit was anticipated and therefore quickly reinvested in government-sanctioned tax shelters, notably his own thoroughbred stock. But this year may be different. Over the weekend, his accountant predicted a $2 million profit from a private January sale to Nelson Bunker Hunt. Stud fees, insurance premiums, and depreciation won't be enough to offset Gentry's yearly income. Suddenly the auction's goal becomes clear; sesamoids or no, sell the Hoist the Flag filly for at least $500,000 or not at all. "Why sell my best filly," he reasons, "when I can keep her and take a capital gain? But it's like winning the battle and losing the war. I can sell her for a sizable profit, which makes me successful, but it all goes to taxes, which makes me a failure. I'm between a rock and a hard spot."

As he enters the air-conditioned pavilion for the sale, Gentry feels the metaphor acutely. He has spent $10,000 preparing each yearling for tonight, and it may not pay off. Surveying the sparse attendance, Gentry grumbles, "Hell, there's not enough people to start a decent poker game." Worse, much of the big money is absent. Last night's sale, a record $41.1 million for 210 yearlings, a fourth straight Keeneland volume record, peaked the prices. While Greek shipping magnate Stavros Niarchos paid $1.7 million for Northern Dancer, it's unlikely he'll repeat such a bid this evening. As buyers funnel into the pavilion, it's obvious they're looking for bargains.

"This is a very tense night for me," Gentry says before sitting down. "I rely heavily on this sale to generate operating revenue for the next year. For me, unlike most of the audience here, thoroughbreds aren't a tax shelter, they're my income. Hoist the Flag filly comes late in the sale. By then I'll have sold eight of my twelve yearlings. If I'm doing too well, I'll decide not to sell her. But if I'm not, I might want every penny of that $500,000."

Two hours earlier Gentry and Robert Meyerhoff met, as is customary, with chief auctioneer Tom Caldwell to set their reserve bid. By making a personal reserve bid of $500,000, Gentry assures the auctioneer of a commission even if prices don't go that high. With this in mind, Caldwell feels confident to start the bidding prices high, thus building the momentum Meyerhoff and Gentry plan to spur with secret bidding of their own. As Gentry explain, "The custom is for the auctioneer to do the bidding for the seller. He has the liberty of the sales area. No one knows who's bidding. So while you don't want anyone to know you're bidding on your own horse, the auctioneer can make it look like the bids are coming from somewhere else in the room."

This strategy is well understood by buyers like

Tom Cooper, who represents a major syndicate known as the British Bloodstock Agency. "Buying is a very confidential business. Very few individuals, no matter how successful, have the personal confidence to go to the last cent. But when a seller knows that an important team is bidding on his animal, it gives him that confidence to have a few more bids, which cost us money. Certain sellers will try to push the price as high as they can. So the less they know about our intentions, the better. We try to disguise our bidding. We've hidden behind pillars; we've gone upstairs and outside. I don't think it works too well. But that's the reason we leave our bidding to the latest moment possible."

As the three Keeneland auctioneers approach the dais, the pavilion lights dim. Only the center light glazes. It illuminates the arc-shaped dais and the semicircular turf just below it with brilliant intensity. In their dark suits and ruffled dress shirts, the auctioneers look strangely operatic. But instead of an aria, a cadence of cash figures sounds from the back of their throats. The bidding has begun.

"What sets the price of a horse at auction," explains Robert Meyerhoff during the first round of bidding, "is two bidders. It only takes two people. That's the miracle." By midpoint of the session, eight of Gentry's yearlings, including the prized Dance Spell colt, have sold for well under hoped-for amounts. Unlike his name, Key to the Mint colt brought a mere $140,000 from bidders. The market is turning against Gentry, and the audience knows it.

"I just don't believe the Hoist the Flag filly is going to be broken down into $10,000 bids." Gentry still sounds hopeful. "I feel she'll go $455,000, $520,000, $540,000. Something of that nature." But in fact, he's worried. While the filly showed well all through the past weekend, today her protective bandages were wrapped too tight. Her ankle is creased. Gentry is worried that the spotlight will accent the fissures.

"Oh, my, ladies and gentlemen," Tom Caldwell says, his voice close to song. "Something special here. A bay filly. What are my bids? Two, two, two, three and a half . . ." Gentry needn't have worried. As she prances in the sawdust turf below the auctioneer's dais, the Hoist the Flag filly is radiant with health. In the bright light, her hip number, 303, glistens as if branded on her flank. Just above her, the bidding box twinkles with digits. "Four, four, four and a quarter. Come on, ladies and gentlemen," Caldwell chides, "this is a stunning filly." Tom Gentry shifts in his seat. He's just given a secret signal to one of the four spot bidders on the floor. He has raised the bid to $450,000 and is now waiting for a late bid from the British Bloodstock syndicate.

"Four fifty. Four fifty. Four fifty." The auctioneer's voice is falling behind, plodding like a cart horse. Gentry suddenly feels the immensity of that long last lap. And then comes another bid. $470,000. Keep bidding, Gentry signals Caldwell. Go for the half million. $475,000. $480,000. $485,000. Suddenly, from across the room, the final bid, $490,000. It's over. Gentry knows: the bid was his own. Robert Meyerhoff, who signaled the bid, will sign the sale ticket. The $490,000, naturally, will not change hands. Gentry must, however, pay Keeneland's 5 percent sales commission, just as he would have had to if the horse had been sold to a real buyer.

*   *   *

THE MARKET'S DECISION has been made. Tom Gentry has just paid $24,500—more than most Americans earn in a year—to learn its verdict. And once it has been issued, there is no appeal. A thoroughbred racehorse at Keeneland gets only one chance, at least until next year.

Yet the lesson has been worth it to Gentry. It is the market, after all, that makes possible his million-dollar annual income. In this sense an auction like Keeneland's is just the tip of an iceberg that rests on a complex system of entrepreneurship and exchange. Racetracks offer aficionados the opportunity to wager on horse races, a big business in itself. The suppliers to this business—the breeders, trainers, stable owners, and stablehands—provide what amounts to raw materials. The investors who buy the horses make it possible for the breeders to stay in business, and provide them with the capital they need to raise topnotch horses. The market's chain works all the way back from the horse lover or gambler who wants to bet on a race to people like Kazuo Nakamura, who gamble on buying a horse.

This of course is precisely the market's genius and the reason it has become the central organizing principle of most industrial economies. Like bettors at a racetrack, consumers making nearly any kind of purchase are merely taking the final step in a long chain of transactions. Along the way, the product being bought may have undergone several transformations, changed hands several times, traveled thousands of miles, and been handled by many different people. All these people have somehow to be induced to cooperate—to pick up where the previous one left off and to pass the product on to the next.

The market is the means to this cooperation. The

orange grower in Florida, for instance, raises oranges with the expectation of making a profit by selling them. The Coca-Cola Company's Minute Maid Division buys oranges in huge quantities, with the expectation of making a profit turning them into frozen concentrate for juice. Railroads and truckers contract to deliver the cans of concentrate to wholesalers or food brokers, who in turn sell them to retailers. In the meantime, speculators and other traders have gambled on orange juice prices in the futures market; advertisers have made money by trumpeting the virtues of Minute Maid as opposed to Snow Crop; lawyers and accountants have been kept busy making sure all the parties get their due. To coordinate all this activity through any device other than the market would require an immense planning apparatus, as the Soviet Union and other socialist nations have discovered. As they also have discovered, it probably wouldn't work as well.

The role of the market thus reflects the complexity of life in an industrial society. In an earlier day, when "markets" were limited to county-fair days or a few firms trading in imported silks and spices, the economy exhibited no such complexity. People grew or fabricated most of what they needed. The few items that were traded probably required no more than a few people's labor to be transformed from raw materials to finished product and to move from original supplier to final customer. An imaginary horse race of that simpler era might bring together a dozen nobles, all of whom lived near each other and raised their own horses, and all of whom were willing to wager a little money on the outcome. Today horse races are held all over, with millions of bets being placed and millions of dollars riding on the various outcomes. Tom Gentry and his colleagues sit at the apex of a system that makes it possible for a racing fan in New York to bet on a horse raised by a stranger in Kentucky and owned by a syndicate of investors from all over the world. Though horse racing of this sort is not an industrial enterprise, it could take place only in a highly organized, complex industrial society—a society that has developed a marketplace capable of handling and coordinating the many transactions on which such a system depends.

As GENTRY and his companions file out of the sale, Nakamura is standing on the ramp leading out of the sales area. He is thumbing through the pocket dictionary Gentry gave him at the party Saturday night. But it would probably take him until next July to locate all the words he needs to explain why he didn't buy Gentry's prize filly. He's waiting to see how well her half-brother will do in his first race three months from now. While he's optimistic the colt was worth the $1.6 million he paid for him, Nakamura doesn't want to set a new record: owning two million-dollar failures from the same family. That would be taking unfair advantage of Japanese politeness. But if the colt wins his European races this fall, as expected to, Nakamura may return and pick up that bay filly.

If she's available, that is. Tom Gentry isn't sure. In a year's time any of a dozen things could be different—the filly's health, Gentry's tax status, the number of other horses he wants to sell, and so on. Besides, like the nobles who once bred horses for pleasure rather than for the market, he has more on his mind than business. "Sometimes," he says as he leaves the Keeneland sales pavilion, "you don't sell your children."

"To ELIMINATE RISK in business is futile," writes the well-known economist and management consultant Peter Drucker. "Risk is inherent in the commitment of present resources to future expectations."

In plain language, Drucker's meaning is simple enough. Any enterprise that sets out to make money is a gamble. Tom Gentry's hopes and fears for his horses at Keeneland represent one such gamble. Levi Strauss's attempt to launch an unusual new line of clothing—the story is told in Chapter Five—represents another.

To most of us, the risks of the business world usually appear no different from the risks run, say, by the New York Yankees. The Yankees can win or lose. A business can make money or lose it. In the long run it can succeed or, like the Washington Senators, it can pass into oblivion.

Yet the reality is both more complex and more interesting. For most businesses, the bottom line is only a summing-up of a dozen different kinds of risk run every day. And the bottom line itself is just a temporary stopping point. Winning one bet means only that you get the opportunity to stay in the game. In business the season never ends.

Nowhere, perhaps, is the pervasiveness of risk so apparent as in the small business. When the small business is a farm—and when the farm's chief crop is a new, largely unknown product with mysterious diseases and uncertain markets—risk becomes simply a fact of life. The story of Marvin Kroeger, who every day deals with risks that would make most of us hang up our spikes, shows just how much it can sometimes take to make a business go.

3. Betting the Farm

1:30 A.M. The air hangs heavy over the Mississippi Delta. The only movement visible to the eye is a curious one: tiny pinpricks of light, darting and scattering like fireflies in the breezeless night. The catfish farmers of Moorhead, Mississippi, are flicking their flashlights nervously over still pond surfaces, looking for something they hope not to see.

At the edge of one 28-acre pond, two flashlights are motionless, their beams focused on the pond's edge. A catfish has come to the surface, gasping for lack of oxygen. Marvin Kroeker and his farm manager, Jimmy Langley, have just caught a glimpse of the unwelcome sight. Quickly Kroeker sweeps his flashlight the length of the pond. As he watches, the one catfish seems to turn into a thousand. Kroeker sucks his breath in. All, he knows, can die in ten minutes. If the pond isn't aerated by then—and if the aeration doesn't bring the water's oxygen level up quickly enough—his $250,000 investment in catfish will literally turn belly up. In a moment Kroeker's whole family is pressed into service. Barn doors open, tractors lumber down the dusty roads that surround the pond. Pumps belch, pipes gurgle, water paddles begin to turn. The pond is a fusillade of spray.

3:30 A.M. Jimmy Langley watches as Kroeker crouches near the edge of the pond and, for the third time in two hours, plunks the oxygen meter into the water. The reading is still dangerously low. Nor is time wholly on his side. At 3:30 A.M., the day's low point where oxygen levels are concerned, pumps and paddles can only do so much. What's needed is sunlight, but the sun won't be up for another couple of hours. In the meantime Kroeker can do little but wait.

Imminent hanging, said Dr. Johnson, concentrates the condemned man's mind most wonderfully. Kroeker's situation is not yet so grim, but the risk he is taking seems to have the same effect. If this pond dies, the others may too. His 500,000 pounds of catfish are his only cash crop, and without them he probably can't repay the $200,000 he borrowed from the bank to get the farm started. Failure to repay the loan might mean losing the farm itself, not to mention the five years of hard work he has already put into building up the business.

The prospects, this Mississippi morning, are not pleasant to contemplate.

ANY ENTREPRENEUR faces risk, from the moment a business is conceived right through to the point when a customer's check is deposited in the bank. The sesamoid problem on Tom Gentry's filly—or something worse—could easily have done in his

$320,000 investment. Wildcatter Bill Brodnax gambled a million dollars of his backers' money on a gas well that could easily turn up dry. Even a giant corporation can't escape risk. When Boeing's president, "Tex" Boullioun, decided to bet that his company's new line of jets could outsell the competition, billions of dollars were at stake. And for Marvin Kroeker, it might be said that life is just one damn risk after another. His story, as it turns out, involves risks that extend well beyond the chance his catfish will die on a hot summer night.

What kind of people are willing to take such risks? For most of us, Webster's definition of risk as "the chance of injury, damage, or loss" is sufficient. Risk is to be avoided; we stick to routines and hedge our bets. Entrepreneurs, however, seem to have a fundamentally different attitude. As a result, what for most of us would be a threat—or, in the event, a gut-wrenching strain—appears to them simply as an opportunity or a problem to be met.

In fact, risk taking appears to be central to a whole cluster of traits that make up what is commonly thought of as the entrepreneurial personality. A profile of risk takers compiled by John Welsh, a professor at Southern Methodist University's Caruth Institute of Owner-Managed Business, reveals a high level of self-confidence, a fierce need to be in control, and a realistic vision of how to achieve various objectives. "Entrepreneurs have a fundamental need to control their own destiny," Welsh says, "and risk taking is the psychological mechanism that allows them to do so. Their self-confidence is commensurate with their control over the decision-making process." Moreover, people with these traits are better able than most to relate risk to achievement.

"They perceive and make meaningful connections between seemingly unrelated variables," says Welsh. "Where others see chaos—and therefore risk—in a business context, they see order because they're always thinking first and last about solutions."

A willingness to take risks, however, is not the same as a willingness to throw caution to the winds. Quite the contrary: entrepreneurs, says Welsh, "don't enter into risk situations unless their perceptions have told them they can win. Or at least have a good shot." Patrick Lyles, a Harvard Business School professor and management consultant, concurs. Entrepreneurial risk takers, he says, can measure risk better than most people and thus minimize it. "Most entrepreneurs don't like risk," he says. "The critical difference is that they understand it. They know how to make it work for them. Instead of intimidating or crippling them, risk energizes them." In *Entrepreneurship: Playing to Win*, Gordon B. Baty echoes Lyles. Risk takers, he argues, aren't really gamblers. They already feel sure that their probable gain will outweigh the probable net costs by a substantial margin.

FOR MOST of his life, Marvin Kroeker had been taking risks. Born on a farm in Nebraska's York County, he might have been the fifth generation of his family to work the rich land of the Corn Belt. In 1957, though, he broke with tradition and moved to Mississippi's Delta country, where he set up an airborne crop-dusting service. Slowly he put together a steady clientele, mostly cotton growers within a ten-mile radius of Moorhead, and he made a good living. "In the 1950s and 1960s," he recalls, "all you had to do was show up. There was more work than I could ever handle."

Then, in 1977, Kroeker learned that the land around his airstrip was up for sale. The prospect of setting up a farm was enticing. It also seemed like a good way to plan for his retirement: a farm enterprise would give him both support and satisfaction once he grew too old to fly. Securing a loan, he bought the land. Those 200 acres—along with his two-story clapboard house, white barn, and corrugated-tin-roofed hangar—was to be Kroeker Farm.

Even in ordinary times no farm can be considered a safe investment. Every ten years the Census Bureau conducts a survey of agriculture in the United States. In 1964 the number of farms in America came to roughly 3.2 million. By 1974 this figure was down to 2.3 million, a drop of 28 percent. For the most part, these statistic indicate hard times for the small farmer: the gradual abandonment of some small farms, the swallowing up of others by larger, more efficient operators. In the same ten-year period the average acreage per farm in the United States rose by roughly one-quarter, from 352 to 440. Mississippi was not immune to these trends. There the number of farms decreased by half, and average acreage rose nearly 65 percent.

There were other changes taking place in Mississippi too, particularly in the Delta. Cotton, once king, was not always profitable and yielded some of its domain to rice and soybeans. Between 1976 and 1978, for example, the acreage given over to cotton in Mississippi decreased 22 percent, while soy acreage rose 17 percent. But the volatile economic climate of the 1970s made all these crops a risky business. Prices could fluctuate dramatically. In 1978 a bushel of soybeans ricocheted between a low of $5.50 and a high of $9.50. In 1980 a pound of cotton bounced between $.50 and $.97. Nor could the weather be counted on to help out. Flying over the drought-stricken cottonfields of Mississippi in 1980, Kroeker could remember similar episodes, stretching back to his Depression-era memories of corn stalks parched by dust and drought. "If you can control the weather," his father had told him, "you can control the profits." Without such control, a farmer's profits are always up for grabs.

There was one kind of farming, however, that Marvin Kroeker thought maybe he could control, and that was catfish. Already this was a fast-growing line of business in the Delta. Conditions in general, notably the area's average 240 days a year of 65-degree-plus weather, were auspicious. And Kroeker's farm was next to ideal. Low-leveled, well-irrigated, rich with heavy clay soil, his 200 acres could easily support a network of ponds and all-weather roads.

Each pond, Kroeker knew, could stock between 5,000 and 6,000 fish per acre. With proper management the ponds, would yield four harvests a year, the largest sometime between March and August. Netted in a huge seine drawn by two tractors, the fish would be weighed and transported to a processing plant thirty miles away. There they would be stunned by a bolt of electricity, gutted, filleted, fast-frozen, and packaged for shipment. At $.65 a pound, Kroeker figured, an acre of catfish would yield an annual net profit of $400, three times that earned for rice or cotton and five times the profit on soybeans. If all went well, his profits might come to $80,000 a year.

*   *   *

ICTALURUS PUNCTATUS, the whiskered fish that seems ubiquitous in the South, is at first glance an unlikely cash crop at all, let alone a source of riches. Ignoble, infamous for its lazy behavior, it has long been part of the region's folklore. In 1673, when Marquette and Joliet made their legendary voyage down the Mississippi, the Indians warned the Jesuit priest and his map-maker companion that the catfish was a "demon whose roar could be heard at a great distance and who would engulf them in the abyss where he dwelt"—or so Marquette recorded in his diary on June 17, the day a large catfish collided with his canoe. In *Life on the Mississippi* Mark Twain remarked on the incident. "I have seen a Mississippi catfish that was more than 6 feet long and weighted 250 pounds; and if Marquette's fish was the fellow to that one, he had a fair right to think the river's roaring demon had come." But Twain also knew that catfish was a docile creature—a river pet for Huck Finn, a quick meal for Tom Sawyer, an emblem of freedom to the slave Jim. In song and story the image that survives is not of the monster but of the slow-moving fish lazing away the day in the South's sun-warmed rivers. As often as not, it's associated too with the barefoot children and run-down shacks of southern rural poverty—a meal for the poor family's table.

Elsewhere, however, less plebeian fish have been moving from their natural habitats to artificial ones. Sea Plantation, Inc., in Salem, Massachusetts, for instance, raises lobster, shrimp, and trout year round. There, water circulates through a variety of biological and ultraviolet filters to sustain desired yields. Similarly, Bob Erskin's Snake River Trout Company— near Buhl, Idaho—produces 12 percent of total U.S.

production on just 10 acres of land. "Aquaculture," as it has come to be known, seems to some a logical answer to the worldwide food problem. High in protein, potentially inexpensive to produce, cultivated fish and shellfish could begin to feed the burgeoning population of Third World countries. Even in today's America they find a ready market. Between 1968 and 1978, fish consumption in the United States shot up 22 percent, as compared with a mere 0.3 percent rise in the consumption of red meat. Frost and Sullivan, an independent industrial research firm in New York, believes that this trend will continue. The market for cultivated fish and shellfish in the United States is projected to triple by 1985, thanks partly to a variety of federal supports provided by the 1980 Aquaculture Act.

For all its down-home reputation, the channel catfish turns out to be a prime candidate for aquaculture. A warm-water fish to begin with, it adapts readily to pond conditions, accepts artificial feed, and tolerates the highly crowded conditions of commercial cultivation. It is also a highly efficient food. High in protein, low in cholesterol, the catfish boasts what farmers call a conversion rate that is little short of spectacular. It takes 2.4 pounds of feed, for instance, to produce a pound of chicken. Ten pounds of feed are needed to produce a pound of beef. Catfish, however, can turn only 1.6 pounds of feed into a pound of fish. At typical prices, that means the catfish can convert 26.5 cents' worth of feed into 65 cents' worth of fish portion.

With possibilities like that, catfish farming was only a matter of time. The first farm appeared in 1965. Since then catfish farming has swelled to encompass some 70,000 acres in 16 states. In 1980 the harvest was 76.7 million pounds, worth more than $54 million to farmers. That, to be sure, was not yet up to the 216.9 million pounds of ocean flounder, worth $82.5 million, harvested in the same year. But catfish is growing fast. Sizable farms can be found in Arkansas, Alabama, Texas, Georgia, Missouri, and even California. In Mississippi's Delta, the nation's catfish axis, pond acreage soared by 50 percent in 1980 and another 40 percent in 1981. Of the nearly 56,000 acres devoted to catfish in Mississippi, almost 95 percent are concentrated in Humphreys and Sunflower counties, the area where Kroeker lives.

As the economics of conventional farming soured, the economics of catfish looked better and better. The story of Dolores and Charles Rowland is typical. Soybean farmers in Humphreys County, the Rowlands went into catfish in the late 1970s. In 1978–79 they made more money from 70 acres of fish than from 1,000 acres of soybeans. During the 1980 drought the fish paid for the loss in soybeans. In 1981 the Rowlands quadrupled their pond acreage and stopped growing soybeans altogether. Dr. John Waldrop, an expert on catfish economics from Mississippi State, estimates that as many as 40 percent of Mississippi farmers were saved from bankruptcy between 1975 and 1981 because of catfish. Charles Estes, a Humphreys County extension agent with the U.S. Department of Agriculture, concurs. "In the 1980 drought," he said, "farmers sat watching their soybeans burn up. But not their catfish. That made catfish look even better." Moreover, catfish and other crops didn't have to be mutually exclusive. Fish farming, Dr. Waldrop points out, replenishes the nitrogen in the soil that rice and beans need. In

Lonoke, Arkansas, one-twelfth of an area previously planted with soybeans was turned over to catfish farming. The next year the small area yielded almost as much soybeans as the rest of the acreage combined, boosting the farmer's income substantially.

High profits and the industry's rapid expansion have begun to catapult catfish out of its regional status into a national market. Already shipped to thirty-six states, including Alaska and Hawaii, catfish is now the focus of an intensive marketing campaign targeted at Sunbelt cities. The Catfish Farmers Association even has its eye on the lucrative but sea-rich Northeast. Their efforts have been sparked by interest on the part of food conglomerates like Standard Brands. In catfish circles, rumors abound that we all may someday be eating McCatfish sandwiches. Even without that kind of boost, the market is projected to more than double by 1985.

So Marvin Kroeker took his $200,000 loan and built 11 ponds, five at 28 acres and six at 10 to 12 acres each. He set aside money for operational costs and high-protein feed. He hired Jimmy Langley, an agriculture instructor at a local junior college, to manage the farm while Kroeker continued to run the crop-dusting service. And he set out to raise his first batch of fish.

Where catfish were concerned, however, his encounters with risk had just begun.

5:30 A.M., dawn. For a moment Kroeker and Langley stand stock-still. There are no fish visible; the danger is over. The sun will soon replenish the pond's oxygen supply. As Langley mounts his feed tractor, Kroeker heaves a heavy sigh of relief. The tension, he knows, will be with him until October, when the last fish is harvested. Tonight the vigil will begin again.

The severest risk in catfish farming is the catfish itself. A highly fragile animal, it can perish in fewer than ten minutes from lack of oxygen. That's why Kroeker and every other catfish farmer in Moorhead keep such careful watch on hot summer nights. Worse, a pond full of dead catfish is useless. The fish at this stage can't even be processed into products like fertilizer or feed. And even if they survive, they may not last until harvest; often they die of stress several weeks later. This means that Kroeker has to feed them, at $1,000 a day, without knowing whether his investment will pay off at all.

Another risk in raising catfish is the range of mysterious diseases they may contract. A hearty scavenger even in a controlled environment like a pond, the catfish is prone to ailments like brown blood, a parasitic illness that permeates its flesh with a musty flavor and renders it unsalable. Catfish, like scrod, must be balanced, almost bland in taste. Sample batches from a farmer's pond are tested by a three-member panel at the processing plant before the fish are purchased. Should his fish be judged "off flavor," a farmer has little recourse. All he can do, if time permits, is change his water, infuse it with chemicals, and hope his fish somehow get back on flavor. So far the experts are baffled by diseases like brown blood. "If someone tells you they're an expert in catfish diseases," cautions Dr. Tom Wellborn, an agricultural specialist at Mississippi State, "run, don't walk, away."

In principle, the most profitable approach to catfish farming is to build large ponds and stock them with a high density of fish—500,000 pounds at a minimum. But the risk in this approach is obvious. The larger the pond, the larger the potential loss. One big pond blighted by brown blood would wipe out a farmer's harvest, cancel his profits, and jeopardize his initial investment.

Faced with risks like these, Kroeker had to make some decisions. In 1979, for example, the fish in his two largest ponds contracted brown blood and were pronounced off flavor by the local processing plant. Kroeker had a month to get the fish back on flavor before harvest. On the advice of a local extension agent, he dumped several tons of salt into the main ponds, a technique that had worked for another farmer. He also decided to change the pond water. But the two moves worked at cross purposes: the water change diluted the strength of the salt, and Kroeker lost his crop. Because he had built several smaller ponds, though, he was able to harvest enough healthy fish to break even.

The next year the fish in Kroeker's two largest ponds again contracted brown blood. To get his fish back on flavor would be costly—and like last year, the attempt might not work at all. Moreover, a $27,000 interest payment on his loan was coming due, and if he were to continue he would have to get the loan extended. Again Kroeker took the risk, persuading his banker that a single healthy crop would enable him to make up the loan. He also contacted Dr. Wellborn and with his help began infusing the pond with chemicals.

The turning point this time came one evening. Kroeker had once wanted to be a doctor and still maintained a modest lab. Examining some gill tissue under a microscope, he found a parasite that might be causing his brown blood problem. His knowledge of pesticides helped him determine what would kill the parasite, and he sprayed the necessary chemicals on his ponds from the air. In the end he couldn't be sure whether the parasite was really the cause of the brown blood. Nor did he know whether his additional spraying or something else was responsible for the improvement. Three weeks later, in any event, his fish were back on flavor. He met his loan extension and was harvesting 500,000 pounds of fish in batches of 20,000 every other week.

IN THE LONG RUN, of course, Marvin Kroeker's fortunes rest only partly on his own hard work and good luck; they rest, too, on the fate of the industry he is now a part of. In this sense raising a healthy crop is only half the battle. A typical catfish farmer, for example, will harvest 50,000 pounds of fish from a single 40-acre pond. Though a few sell direct to "live haulers," as catfish transporters are known, most sell to processing plants. The plants, which are at the heart of the catfish marketing network, buy the fish and process it, then sell it to a variety of local distributors. These include restaurants, food chains, and institutional buyers like hospitals and schools.

Until 1974, when catfish were officially declared an industry, markets developed faster than the plants could serve them. Then the number of plants began to catch up, in some cases even exceeding the market's capacity to absorb their output. At this point farmers and processors alike found themselves victims of the industry's uncoordinated marketing system. In August, the height of the harvest season, processing plants operated at capacity. That glutted the market, driving prices down, and left some farmers no choice but to hold their fish until the plants could handle them. By then the fish might have ballooned to three pounds each, too big to be sold. At other times of the year, however, the plants couldn't get enough fish to operate at capacity. Plant operators frequently lost money in these periods; worse, they sometimes were unable to supply their regular customers. "We've found we can sell all the fish we can produce," said Mark Freeman, president of the Catfish Farmers Association. "The real pity is reneging on already established markets—grocery and restaurant wholesalers. It's much harder establishing business a second time around."

Recently the industry has developed a sophisticated netting system allowing fingerlings to slip back into the water, thus aiding year-round harvesting. It also has stepped up its marketing efforts. Processing plants have established distribution networks in Chicago, New York, and other northern cities as well as in the South, and one industry association collects $2 a ton from farmers to pay for advertising campaigns targeted at cities with established distributors. The ads—featuring, for example, tuxedo and chiffon-dressed elegantes dining on catfish—are designed as much to counter the catfish's image problem as to tout its virtues. If catfish are to catch on, the theory runs, they will have to overcome their reputation as the fish you eat when you can't afford anything else.

Will it work? Farmers like Kroeker believe that the cheap, high-protein fish speaks for itself—and Tommy Taylor, a Humphreys County extension agent, quips, "It's so good, it'll make you slap your grandma." But poet Roberta Spear probably captures the Northerner's attitude best in her damning-with-faint-praise poem in a March 1981 issue of *The New Yorker:* "By 6 A.M. the catfish/freshened on ice/have lost their pallor/and look like something/you'd want to eat." No one knows whether that attitude can be changed. A possibility to watch for is that the catfish, like an ambitious ingenue making her debut, will adopt a stage name. Crispy Southern Fish or Delta Dover Sole might sell to the kind of people who wouldn't be caught eating a catfish. Maybe, of course, it will catch on all by itself, helped by a sluggish economy and by Americans' evident desire to eat more fish and less red meat. If that happens, Kroeker's position will be a little more secure than it is at the moment.

In the meantime he has to face a double problem. He first has to manage his business successfully: obtain his capital, construct and stock his ponds, raise a healthy crop. That alone requires a combination of luck, persistence, and effort that might be enough to daunt most people. He then has to hope that the market will hold up—that processors will buy his fish at a decent price and be able to sell them at a profit. That part of his business is every bit as important as the first part, yet it is largely beyond his control.

KROEKER'S DILEMMA is not unique. Any entrepreneur faces a difficult enough task assembling or managing a business and getting the products out to buyers. Whether the industry will thrive or die out, and whether any individual entrepreneur will turn out to be in the right place at the right time, are matters that are equally problematic but less predictable. The catfish business, to be sure, is riskier than most, simply because it is so new. But no business is guaranteed a market forever, and no enterprise can count itself safe from competition, bad luck, or the vagaries of taste and buying habits. Virtually anyone who proposes to go into business has to be prepared to confront these risks.

Yet if risk is endemic to the market system, so is it an indispensable element of the way the market works. In nonmarket economies—the world of the feudal lord and serf, for instance, or a highly planned socialist economy—business is undertaken and transactions completed because things have always been that way, or because the government orders it. Risk is therefore less of a factor. But there is also less assurance that the economy will actually be responding to what consumers want and need. Because the market is a system of *free* enterprise, and because no one can predict what consumers and entrepreneurs will freely choose to do, risk in the marketplace is inevitable.

For his part, Marvin Kroeker isn't worried. He has kept his product healthy in recent years, watching his ponds' oxygen levels with all-night vigils when necessary. In 1982 he planned to increase his stock from 45,000 fingerlings per acre to 60,000, and he was optimistic about the future. He had not, to be sure, made much money yet: the farm at last report was just about breaking even. But that didn't faze him. Success, in Kroeker's view, was "being able to pay your debts."

Gradually the market will reach its decisions. Consumers will decide whether they do or do not like catfish. Processors and brokers will find they can or cannot make a go of it, and farmers will decide to stock more or less fish, depending on how many they can sell. Through all these decisions the market will ensure that about as many fish get produced as people are ready and able to buy. In the meantime, though, Kroeker, like every other participant in the industry, has to live with the uncertainty and has to be willing to take the risks involved. If they weren't, neither the catfish industry nor any other business would ever get off the ground.

STORIES LIKE Marvin Kroeker's could be told in a thousand different settings. The risks he faces in the marketplace are the very stuff of the entrepreneur's world. They are the challenges any business has to confront and overcome.

In the chapters that follow, we will take a closer look at three of these challenges. To operate a business, entrepreneurs and companies must first raise money. Then they must develop a product for which there is a market. Finally they must sell the product. In principle, simple enough. But none of these steps is as easy as it sounds.

Take, for example, finance, the subject of the next chapter. As first-year business students learn, there are three ways to raise capital. You can use your own money. You can borrow the money, from the First National Bank or from your Aunt Bessie. Or you can sell shares in your company, a process that provides what is known as equity capital. The real world, however, is seldom so cut-and-dried as this outline would suggest. Assembling a financing package can be a challenge to the most sophisticated executive. And it frequently involves a dramatic story, with entrepreneurs and investors alike wondering if the deal can be assembled—and once assembled, if it will pay off.

Few stories, indeed, are as dramatic as John Z. DeLorean's. DeLorean is a lean, hard-driving engineer who tried against all the odds to start an automobile company. It was a job that involved fitting hundreds of pieces together. But the first piece, and in many ways the biggest one, was finding the money. How DeLorean did it makes for an interesting case study, not only about finance in general but about the particular political and economic environments in which today's innovators must do their wheeling and dealing.

4. Making a Deal

A COUPLE OF YEARS ago, a small group of acquaintances in northern California got together to form a new automobile club. The car each of them owned was, to put it mildly, unusual. A high-performance sports car, it sold for about $26,000. Its body, designed by the Italian stylist Giorgetto Giugiaro, who also designed Maseratis and Ferraris, featured a fiberglass underbody and a unique stainless-steel skin. The car's doors opened upward rather than outward, giving it the effect of a seagull in flight. With leather upholstery, high seats, and a space-age dash console, it was, as *Fortune* put it, a "sports car for gentlemen."

Only one thing concerned the car enthusiasts in the new club. Shortly after the organization was formed, the company that manufactured the stylish automobiles looked as if it might be going out of business. Club members worried, according to *For-*

tune, about the availability of parts and the cost of repairs. But they also began to think that things might not turn out so badly after all. If production ceased altogether, the car could become an instant classic, its value driven up by scarcity. "If the ball game is over, I'm going to put the car up on blocks in the garage and leave it for a couple of years," club president Gene Daly told a reporter. "Then I'm going to advertise it in the *Wall Street Journal* and sell it for 50-K to some guy in the Midwest."

THE AUTOMOBILE Daly and the others owned was the DMC-12, the first and apparently the only product of the DeLorean Motor Company. The firm wasn't very old before it ran into trouble: it began shipping cars from its Belfast (Ireland) plant in 1981, and by early 1982 was in receivership. What was surprising, however, wasn't the company's troubles, for building and selling a new automobile may be one of the hardest tasks an entrepreneur could set for himself. The surprising part was that the company got as far as it did. Somehow, company founder John Z. DeLorean, a man who would later be arrested on a charge of trafficking in cocaine, had raised the money to design a new automobile, to construct a new manufacturing plant, and to assemble a network of dealers capable of marketing the vehicle once it was produced. By the time he was through, the bill for all this was well over $200 million. Nearly all of it was raised on the strength of an idea alone, and on the reputation of the man who proposed to turn the idea into reality.

John Zachary DeLorean, the son of a Detroit foundry worker, had a meteoric career at General Motors—so dramatic that he was said to be the model for the character Adam Trenton in Arthur Hailey's best-selling novel *Wheels.* An engineer by training, he was recruited by Pontiac in 1956 from the now-defunct Packard Motor Company. Twelve years later he became, at age forty, the youngest head of Pontiac ever. He performed so well there that GM put him in charge of Chevrolet, the company's biggest division. Again he was a success, and in 1973 the company named him vice-president and group executive in charge of all car and truck divisions in North America. His salary—in 1973 dollars—was $650,000.

Then, that same year, the man everyone thought was in line for the presidency of General Motors shocked the industry by resigning. Rumors abounded, but both GM and DeLorean stayed mute on the reasons for the resignation. DeLorean's version surfaced in 1979, written up in a book by J. Patrick Wright called *On a Clear Day You Can See General Motors.* Billed as John Z. DeLorean's story, the book was printed at Wright's own expense, without DeLorean's authorization. But DeLorean didn't disown it either.

DeLorean, the book made plain, had gradually fallen out with the company's top executives, housed on the fourteenth floor of GM headquarters at 800 West Grand Boulevard in Detroit. One reason, it seemed, was his flashy life-style. Another was the fact that he didn't think they knew what they were doing up on the fourteenth floor. "As an engineer who spent the first 20 years of his professional life designing automobiles and their components," he wrote later, "I have very strong feelings that the control of our industry must return to the technical side. The financial and marketing people have failed."

DeLorean was evidently one of a kind, a distinct personality with a freewheeling style that worked well on the divisional level but wouldn't blend in on the fourteenth floor. Some suspect he couldn't stand not sticking out. Or like Bill Brodnax, he may simply not have been satisfied with the promise of a fat and comfortable job.

At age forty-eight DeLorean took a one-year appointment as head of the National Alliance of Businessmen, a job-finding organization set up under the Johnson administration. It was a sinecure, some thought, but that didn't matter: DeLorean had other things on his mind. If the gray-suit set at GM didn't know how to build a car, perhaps he did. Gradually an idea took shape. He would design, build, and market a special car, a car like none ever built, one that would make John Z. DeLorean the first successful automobile entrepreneur since Walter Chrysler in 1925. He put together a small company known as the John Z. DeLorean Corporation and began work. Later, in a jibe at Detroit-style profiteering and disregard for safety, he would characterize his firm as "the ethical car company."

From the beginning DeLorean planned a two-seat sports model. His theory was that he would have a better chance of succeeding with a unique and relatively expensive car than with a mass-market sedan. He suspected from his experience at Chevrolet that there was a sizable unfilled demand in this class and price range. Corvette, at $14,000, had widened its share of the GM product mix from 6.3 percent in 1972 to 12.4 percent in 1977. More important, all 40,000 Corvettes built every year sold out. "In fact," DeLorean recalled, "we had to send back over 8,000 orders a year because we couldn't deliver them."

*   *   *

DELOREAN WAS sure he could solve the problems of design, engineering, manufacturing, and marketing. But would he get the chance to? His first big problem was money—and skepticism on the part of potential backers that the idea could work.

Typically, any entrepreneur has three potential sources of capital available to start a new business. One is his or her own money. Rarely can a firm be started without an individual investment, for even if other capital is available, the backers will want to be sure that the entrepreneur has a stake in the firm. By the same token, though, the founder's own money is seldom sufficient. Those who propose to begin a new venture nearly always have to seek outside financing.

This financing falls into two categories. One is what's known as equity capital, ordinarily represented by stock ownership. The equity investor puts in money to become a part owner of the firm. If the enterprise is successful, the investor will share in its profits, and the stock will be worth considerably more than when it was bought. If the firm fails, the investor loses out. Equity investment in a new company, naturally, is a high-risk proposition. Equity investment in an established company need involve no more risk than a fall of a few points in the firm's stock price.

The second category of financing is called debt financing. Debt finance can be a simple loan, as from a bank or a friend. It can also take the form of bonds, through which a company borrows money from anonymous investors. New firms, of course, usually have to borrow from individuals or local banks who can acquaint themselves with the entrepreneur's track record and business plans. Large, well-established firms can borrow simply by issuing debentures on the bond market. Unlike equity capital, where investors earn only a share of the company's profits, debt capital carries a commitment to repay the lender both the principal and a fixed rate of interest. A company's *debt-to-equity ratio*, a figure often discussed in the financial pages, reflects its relative dependence on the two forms of finance.

A particular form of equity financing is provided by what are known as venture-capital firms. These are partnerships, typically, that pool investment funds for early-stage financing of new enterprises. The firm's staff investigates fledgling companies, or entrepreneurs with ideas, deciding whether or not to offer the firm's backing. If the decision is favorable, the venture-capital company may pour many millions of dollars into a business and may even wind up providing extensive management or marketing consultation. The venture capitalists' objective, however, is not usually to stay involved in running a company. Rather it is to see a company to the point where it has a healthy balance sheet and can "go public," or sell shares on the open market. At that point the venture firm's investment should be worth many times its original value.

Few enterprises can qualify for venture-capital financing. Venture capitalists seek companies in new, expanding markets, with prospects for growth of at least 20 percent a year. They tend therefore to focus on modern, high-tech industries. They also seek entrepreneurs with proven track records, in order to minimize their risk. And they will seldom consider a firm for financing that does not have a potential market of at least $50 million.

*   *   *

RAISING MONEY for a new venture, in short, can be hard. Raising money for a new automobile company must have seemed well-nigh impossible, even to John DeLorean. Recent history was not encouraging. The Tucker Torpedo, introduced in 1946, flopped after eating up $40 million. Henry Kaiser's auto company, manufacturers of the Kaiser, the Fraser, and the Henry J, lasted just ten years, from 1945 to 1955. When it folded, the loss was calculated at $100 million. The most recent example was the celebrated case of Malcolm Bricklin, a thirty-three-year-old millionaire who tried to set up his own sports car company in Canada in 1974. It too fell apart, after turning out only 3,000 cars.

Starting a company capable of building modern automobiles is no simple task. Henry Ford's Model T and Model A were relatively simple machines, but today's cars have 15,000 parts. They include systems ranging from the engine and transmission to brakes, suspension, and electronic controls. No manufacturers build all these systems themselves. Instead they have to procure them from other plants, get them to the assembly plant on time, and make sure they all fit together. The final product then has to stand up against all the other models on the market—vehicles built by companies like Volkswagen, Toyota, and GM, all with established facilities and well-trained work forces.

But that's just the beginning of the would-be entrepreneur's problems. The real trouble with creating a new car company is that you can't start small. The capital costs of designing, building, and marketing a new car are so high that a plant must be ready to produce and sell a lot of cars. GM's new Lake

Orien, Michigan, assembly plant, for example, is
expected to cost some $400 million. The company
estimates that it cost $3 billion to design, build, and
market its popular X-body series (which includes
the Chevrolet Citation) and nearly $5 billion to cre-
ate its new J series. GM, of course, can afford such
outlays. Last year it borrowed $2 billion on the
overseas capital markets, raising its long-term debt
to $3.8 billion. It also raised $303 million from
selling stock, $217 million from selling property,
and $424 million on loans from the General Motors
Acceptance Corporation, its unconsolidated financing subsidiary. Reflecting on GM's situation, De-
Lorean observed: "When you work for General
Motors and you want to build a new foundry for
$500 million, you fill out a form and send it
away. You might get a phone call or two, or you
might not. Then within a few months this docu-
ment comes back with 100 signatures on it which
says go spend $600 million."

Working for himself instead of GM, DeLorean was
in a rather different situation. He knew he would
have to build thousands of cars a year to make a
profit. He knew too—even then—that in the long
run his company would have to broaden its product
line to succeed. At the same time he had nothing to
offer investors but an idea. He had no collateral for
their loans, no plant or equipment they could "buy"
with an equity investment.

To be sure, there are times when little more than
an idea is enough. Take, for example, the case of
Genentech, a San Francisco company experimenting
with recombinant DNA technology to make synthetic insulin, growth hormones, and the anti-cancer
drug interferon. Genentech is small: its 1979 sales

came to only $3.4 million. But in 1980 it decided to issue a million shares of stock—15 percent of its total number of shares—for public sale. On the issue's first day, the asking price was $35 a share. Ninety minutes from the opening bell it climbed to $86; by the end of the day it was $71, the largest single-day increase for a new issue in almost twenty years. Selling the issue raised $35 million for the company, all on the anticipation of future profitability.

John DeLorean couldn't count on quite the same degree of enthusiasm from would-be shareholders as Genentech. David Healy, a respected auto industry analyst with the investment firm of Drexel Burnham Lambert, said: "When people ask my advice about investing in Mr. DeLorean's venture, I tell them to put their money into wine, women, and song. They'll get the same return, and they'll have more fun." At some point DeLorean would have to issue shares on the open market to meet his venture's continuing capital needs. But he couldn't start off this way simply because his enterprise was too risky. His initial prospectus, aimed at private investors, warned that investment should be considered only by those "who can afford a total loss."

So, like most entrepreneurs, he started with his own money, though exactly how much is not known. Then he put together a limited partnership with a group of Merrill Lynch executives, raising $472,500. He raised $8.6 million more through a unique arrangement with the 345 U.S. auto dealers whom he had signed up to carry his product. The dealers each bought $25,000 worth of stock, issued a $100,000 letter of credit, and agreed to buy between 50 and 150 cars.

More investors: Johnny Carson bought $500,000

in equity. The Canadian investment bank of Wood Gundy, Limited, bought $1 million. Oppenheimer & Co., a venture-capital firm, put together another limited partnership deal for $20 million, with each investor contributing a minimum of $150,000. All told, DeLorean raised some $35 million through this motley mix of initiatives. Necessarily, he traded in large measure on his own prestige, his salesmanship, and the fantasy appeal of the car he proposed to build. One of his major investors, Merrill Lynch president Paul Schneider, first had misgivings about the risk, but his confidence in DeLorean's drive and experience overcame his doubts. When he saw a prototype of DeLorean's car, the DMC-12, he said, "I was so excited I felt like a little boy at F.A.O. Schwarz."

But $35 million was still not enough. The breakthrough came when DeLorean realized that conventional financing methods would never do the trick—and that he had something to offer besides a potential return on investment. That something was jobs. Like Lee Iacocca of Chrysler, who convinced Congress to provide his company with $1.2 billion in loan guarantees partly to save 140,000 Chrysler jobs, DeLorean began to think politically. He was encouraged to do so by the interest that officials from various states and countries were showing in his plant. Puerto Rico called. So did George Wallace, who wanted him to build his plant in Alabama. So too did the Northern Ireland Development Agency, an arm of the British government, which had been looking for job-creating enterprises to relieve the 17 percent unemployment rate in the violence-wracked province.

In 1978, DeLorean signed an agreement. The British government would put up $130 million in loans, cash, and equity and in return would get what DeLorean termed "a very substantial equity interest" in the company. DeLorean would build his plant in Dunmurry, a depressed district in West Belfast. He would hire 2,600 workers, equally divided between Protestants and Catholics, and would pay the British government $398 per car on the first 90,000 built and $187 a car for ten years thereafter.

For Britain it was one of the more expensive job-creating deals in history: an estimated $50,000 per job. For DeLorean it was a brilliant piece of financial maneuvering. The company that could not go public had nonetheless obtained a kind of "public" financing. A venture that was deemed too risky by many potential investors was adopted by one big investor, the British government, because of what it could offer right now. With the government on board, DeLorean could build his factory and put people to work.

DELOREAN'S JOB now was to bring the venture to the point where it could churn out 18,000 to 20,000 cars a year for the American market. He would have to slingshot the company into profitability on this initial package of investments, then go public for the financing he would later need to diversify and expand. As the inevitable problems mounted, though, financing continued to be an issue.

DeLorean's company had to build a new assembly plant and hire and train a work force. That by itself might have been challenge enough. It also had to make the arrangements with other companies to produce various parts of the car. The body was to be engineered by Lotus Cars, Ltd., of England, for $18.8

million. The engines would come from Renault, the air-conditioning from GM. A variety of plants in Northern Ireland, employing 3,000 workers all told, would supply parts for DeLorean's assembly line. Not surprisingly, there were delays and foul-ups. Engineers ran into problems with the car's crash resistance and construction materials. The engine deal with Renault got snarled up, and the contractor hit some snags in building the assembly plant. Each month of delay cost DeLorean $600,000. By the time production began, the car that was to cost $15,000 was now projected to sell for something more like $25,000. And DeLorean's market research had indicated that each price increase significantly decreased the number of prospective buyers.

With each new setback, DeLorean went back to the British government, just as Iacocca had done in the United States, and asked for more cash. He always played the political card: if the government didn't come through, he would have to close the factory, putting 2,400 people out of work and possibly exacerbating the tense political situation in the province. There was a lot at stake for both sides. As one Northern Ireland observer put it: "DeLorean has become a symbol of what could happen here if the killing could somehow be stopped. If DeLorean can't make it, that will be a symbol of defeat." On the basis of such logic, the British government continued to put up money. Before it was finished, it had lent or guaranteed $150 million.

But each new arrangement also brought new criticism, from press and politicians alike. The political situation was complicated enough: James Callaghan's Labour government had made the deal, but Margaret Thatcher's Conservative government was left holding the checkbook. The Sunday *Times* fumed in 1980, "Is John Zachary DeLorean worth a 50 million pound gamble with your money?" Tory members of Parliament growled on the floor of the House of Commons that the government was throwing away a fortune on a "bunch of American con men." Said James Prior, Secretary for Northern Ireland and a staunch Conservative, "I have never been optimistic." Knowing that the British government couldn't be counted on indefinitely, DeLorean planned a $28 million public issue of stock for the summer of 1981. Some 2.25 million shares of a new firm, DeLorean Motors Holding Company, would be offered at $12.50 a share. Part of the proceeds, said *Fortune*, "would be spent to begin buying out the members of the limited partnership, who stood to reap almost one-quarter of the company's profits; the rest of the cash would be working capital. None of it would have gone to John DeLorean, but his 49% interest in the new company would have a paper value of $120 million."

The plan ran into obstacles. The British government, which had to approve it, dragged its feet. Allegations of management wrongdoing, none of them substantiated, turned up in the press. Eventually the offering was postponed indefinitely.

Nevertheless, in May 1981, only eight months behind schedule, the first cars began to roll off the assembly line. By November DeLorean Motor Company was building 80 DMC-12s a day, employing 2,400 workers, and shipping cars to the United States. "The company has weathered the last 11 months reasonably well," said *Business Week*, "and DeLorean has left little doubt about which way he is aiming the company. With production already at its target rate of 80 cars a day, or about 20,000 cars per year, the company claims to be making an operating profit."

"The first phase of this successful enterprise has now been completed," DeLorean announced. "What remains is the all-important test in the marketplace."

THE RESULTS OF the test were not long in coming:

LONDON, February 19, 1982(AP)—The British Government declared U.S.-run DeLorean Motor Company in Northern Ireland insolvent today. Receivers said they hoped to restructure the company to keep it in business and salvage some jobs. "We have lost a great deal of money," said Northern Ireland Secretary James Prior after announcing in the House of Commons the government's decision not to invest more money in the business."

Shortly before, DeLorean had gone to the British government for one more round of financing, asking for $70 million in export credits to pay for shipping cars to the United States. The government refused and asked the accounting firm of Coopers & Lybrand to inspect the company's books. When the accountants reported that DeLorean's operations were insolvent, the government put the firm into receivership.

This was the start of a series of troubles. DeLorean set about looking for a rescuer: people or institutions willing to put in substantial amounts of additional capital. First he borrowed $5 million from Citibank in New York and put the money into the Northern Ireland manufacturing plant. Under the terms of the receivership, this act relieved his New York operations of the obligation to pay off a $70 million loan used to construct the plant. Then he set about looking for more money. For a while it seemed possible that Budget Rent-a-Car, a division of the TransAmerica corporation, would buy 1,000 unsold DMC-12s for rental to customers. Then DeLorean announced that he had unnamed investors lined up to put in an additional $35 million. Meanwhile, however, the Bank of America—DeLorean's largest creditor—sued the company for alleged default on an $18 million loan. That suit was eventually settled, but the Budget deal didn't come through. By the beginning of summer 1982 DeLorean had been unable to announce firm financing. In October the British Government decided the venture was hopeless and closed the plant permanently. Only hours later DeLorean was arrested and charged with possession of 60 pounds of cocaine. He allegedly had turned to drug dealing in a last-ditch attempt to save the company.

What went wrong? According to *Fortune*, part of the problem lay in management errors. The company's marketing department, for example, said it could sell at most 12,000 DMC-12s a year. But DeLorean himself "aimed higher," at the 20,000 goal reported by *Business Week*, and "cranked the plant up to 80 cars a day." Again the marketing department said it couldn't sell that many. Finance worried about the overhead, and manufacturing worried about the influx of untrained workers. "But DeLorean kept the plant going at high speed. 'I guess we got carried away,' he says now."

Another part of the problem, ironically, was financial. DeLorean had raised $200 million, but it wasn't enough. According to a report in *The New*

York Times, the company "had never built up any working capital and had been operating from hand to mouth since its inception. . . ." When the receivers came in, DeLorean told the *Times*, the firm had simply run out of cash. The shortage of capital made it seem as if more money might rescue the firm and accounted for DeLorean's efforts in that direction after receivership was declared.

But much of the trouble was more basic still. What finally did in John DeLorean's $200 million dream was, ironically, something wholly out of his control: the worst recession in the American auto business in fifty years. DeLorean was, for the most part, skillful and lucky. He advertised heavily, and there was indeed some pent-up demand for the long-awaited, much publicized new car. But sales, after a strong start, slumped badly. By early spring 1982 fewer than 5,000 of the first 7,000 cars built had been sold, and the ones on the market were reportedly being discounted. Selling an untested car for $26,000 might be a good test of salesmanship in any market. Selling one for that much in the market conditions of 1982 in the United States, when not even GM and Ford could sell their cars, proved well-nigh impossible. Tim Klapp, a DeLorean dealer in Beverly Hills, put the problem succinctly. "It's very difficult," he said, "to sell people a $26,000 new idea."

What is surprising, in retrospect, is that so many sophisticated people believed that DeLorean's dream really could succeed. Many who knew him, like Merrill Lynch's Schneider, seemed to think he could do anything he set out to do. Bunkie Knudsen, the former GM executive who had hired DeLorean in 1956, said, "If anybody can do it, he can." And

James Wallace, a Chase Manhattan banker who had worked with DeLorean at GM, put it this way: "Everybody who's ever tried it has failed. But they don't know John. I'd almost say, only he could do it." DeLorean capitalized on this reputation, and shrewdly marketed himself along with his car. His own name graced both car and company. He appeared in the ads in jeans and rough shirt, leaning on the car, with the slogan "Live the Dream." In interviews he played up the purity of his motives. "I'm fifty-six," he told one reporter. "By the time this thing gets off the ground I'll be sixty-five. You don't do this sort of thing for the money, you do it because you love it."

In the end, love was not enough. Neither, as it turned out, was a unique capital package that probably only John DeLorean could have put together. Unable to sell stock publicly and unable to borrow the kind of money needed, he had to rely on a combination of unusual financing methods to get the money he required. These included partnerships, investment and in-kind contributions from dealers, and eventually direct assistance from the British government. He capitalized, literally, on all the benefits his firm could offer—cars, profits, and jobs. He also took advantage of the element of fantasy, both in his own plans and in his appeals to investors.

Was DeLorean unrealistic? Probably—and probably he needed to be so to get as far as he did. "Those involved in starting a new venture," writes William H. Shames in his book *Venture Management*, "have a need to believe and often do not want to be confused by the facts. In a sense, this must be the case, because few new ventures would be started if the entrepreneur-inventor or the investors were totally realistic. The mountain has to be climbed because it's there. Either you understand that or you don't."

Some reactions to DeLorean's troubles indicate how important this idea is to the business world in general. A McKinsey & Company consultant hired to evaluate DeLorean for the British government described DeLorean's accomplishments to *Fortune* this way: "Here was a man who came along promising to jump 9 feet. He only jumped 7 feet, 6 inches, which happens to be a world record. Now everyone's saying, 'But he's 1½ feet short.' " Even after the arrest, DeLorean's chief engineer said of him, "He believed he could do anything."

Until then, DeLorean's effort had had its poignant moments. When he returned to New York from London, for example, exhausted from having negotiated the terms of the receivership, he found a letter containing a $20 check. The sender, according to *The New York Times*, had enclosed the check with a letter saying, "I am sending you some money to put into the company. It's not much, but I am in the process of becoming an entrepreneur and it takes money."

"A grin spread across his face," the *Times* wrote, "as Mr. DeLorean said: 'If I can get every American to send me $10, I'd be out of trouble. It's a new financing program.' "

THE MARKET, as John DeLorean discovered, can be a fickle mistress. No one can predict what consumers will choose to buy, if only because consumers themselves don't always know. The best-laid plans—to buy a DMC-12, a new dress, or a house in Florida—can go awry when the grim realities of economic life intrude. The resulting uncertainty makes life harsh for the entrepreneur.

Even for an established company, the business of putting a new product on the market can be something of a shell game. A firm needs to ascertain—or guess at—its customers' wants and tastes. It needs to create and sell a product that will fit that demand, and to do so at a price that is not beyond the buyer's reach. Finally it needs to do all these things better and quicker than the competition. Getting to the market with just what consumers want doesn't do much good if someone else got there first.

This problem of product development may not seem important to a huge, profitable, and well-known firm like Levi Strauss, the San Francisco-based clothing manufacturer. But even a company like Levi can't rest on its laurels. Already the business on which it made its name—blue jeans—is not as profitable as it once was. And no one can predict what the next generation of consumers will want to wear or indeed what the present generation will wear as it grows older. So Levi, like every other company, has to try to stay one jump ahead of the marketplace.

In the next chapter Levi tries to do just that. The story of one new product—an important one to Levi, and one whose success was by no means assured—shows some of the opportunities and some of the pitfalls facing a big company as it diversifies. In the process, it shows that a big company and a small one have something in common.

Both must face the uncertainty of the marketplace. And both, in the last analysis, can only hope that what they're selling is something consumers will want to buy.

5. Finding the Fit

THE SCENE is an ordinary-looking room, Corporate Modern in style, white-walled and windowless. Around a table in the middle sit six well-dressed young men, their eyes trained on the discussion leader, Malcolm Baker. Baker periodically stabs at his flip chart, asking the group questions, prodding for more complete answers. In an adjoining room sit four others, three men and a woman, watching the discussion intently through one-way glass that looks like a smoky mirror from the discussion-group side. The atmosphere in this observation booth is light: the four talk and joke as they watch. But every now and then conversation stops as they strain to catch one of the discussants' answer to a key question. This is not, evidently, an interrogation for espionage. But it doesn't quite seem to be a parlor game either.

In fact the scene is an exercise in the arcane field of corporate market research. The six around the table are a "focus group" of representative consumers, chosen for their tastes and clothes-buying habits and paid $20 apiece to share their views with Baker, a research consultant. The observers represent Levi Strauss & Company, the world's largest apparel manufacturer. The company has decided to introduce a new line of men's clothing, aimed at buyers very much like those Baker is now talking with. The four observers—a group that includes Peter Haas, great-great-grandnephew of Levi Strauss himself—is in charge of getting the new line from the drawing board to the department-store rack.

The Tailored Classic, as the new line is known, is a radical departure for Levi. It will include dress slacks, sport coats, and three-piece suits, in wool and wool-blended fabrics, all with a classic, conservative cut. Compared with similar items from a men's clothing store, the Tailored Classic line will be inexpensive, particularly since it is designed to require no hand-tailoring. Compared with Levi's usual fare of jeans and casual wear, however, the Tailored Classic is costly. It represents the company's first attempt to go after the lucrative mid-to-upper range of the men's clothing market. If Levi can sell sport coats and suits with the same success it has sold jeans, the profits will be substantial. More important, a new segment of the marketplace will be opened up to Levi as store buyers and consumers alike come to identify the company name with higher-quality, dressier clothing. With so much at stake, it is not surprising that Baker's discussion group seems like something more than idle chatter. When one of the participants offers an opinion about what kind of clothes he likes and why, the four from Levi

Strauss react like the passersby in an E. F. Hutton ad. They listen.

Yet though the question of the moment is simple enough—is the Tailored Classic a product consumers will buy?—the more interesting questions have to do with why this group was assembled in the first place. Levi is, after all, a $2-billion-a-year company, a firm whose name is virtually synonymous with the kind of pants most favored by young (and not so young) men and women all over the world. Why should it diversify at all? And if it does decide to bring out new lines, doesn't it have the reputation, skills, and pure economic muscle to sell just about anything it wants to? These questions have answers—some rooted in the unusual history of Levi Strauss & Company itself, some in a peculiar set of problems almost any company must confront when it tries to open up new markets for itself. The riddle of product development, of finding the fit between what a company can do and what a group of consumers might want, is one that even corporations as phenomenally successful as Levi must address. It is not one that most enterprises find easy to solve.

LEVI STRAUSS arrived in New York from Europe in 1847. A Bavarian Jew in his early twenties, he spoke no English and could claim no trade. Three years later he followed the gold rush to California, planning on selling dry goods—especially tent canvas—to miners. Since there wasn't much of a demand for tents, Strauss took the canvas and stitched together some pairs of heavy-duty pants, durable enough for mud-splattered miners. The pants sold, and Strauss made more. Soon traveling salesmen were packing them into trunks and piling the trunks on wagons headed into the frigid mining country of the Sierra Nevada.

With the money he made from such trips, Strauss opened up a small dry-goods shop in 1857. Open six days a week, twelve hours a day, the store was the first of several that bore his name. Ships arriving in San Francisco's harbor supplied him with inventory—cotton yardage one week, men's shirts the next. Sales boomed, and Levi Strauss & Company was one of the few dry-goods establishments to survive the earthquakes and financial tremors that shook San Francisco between 1855 and 1870.

In 1872 Strauss got a letter from a Reno tailor named Jacob Davis who had patented a rather curious invention. When customers brought pants with ripped pockets to him for repair, Davis fixed them by anchoring the pockets with copper rivets. He knew he had discovered something: "The secratt of them Pents," he wrote to Strauss, "is the Rivits I put in those Pockets." And he offered to sell Levi Strauss a half-share in the rights to his pants for $68, the cost of a patent application.

Strauss bought, and Davis moved to San Francisco. "Within a few years," write Milton Moskowitz and his colleagues in the book *Everybody's Business*, "the company was turning out a model that has remained virtually unchanged until the present day: the '501 Double X Blue denim waist overall.'" By 1873 the firm had sold 5,875 riveted pants, vests, coats, and jumpers. By 1877 Levi Strauss & Company, now employing some 250 machine operators, was manufacturing 100,000 garments annually. In the years that followed, Strauss himself grew rich and prominent, an important man in San Francisco. He died in 1902, leaving most of his $6 million estate to four nephews.

The firm continued to prosper, both as a manufacturer and as a wholesaler, under the nephews' management. The 501 Double X was rapidly becoming what would now be called a cult item, but the cult was small: farmers, miners, lumbermen. In 1920 one Homer Campbell of Constellation, Arizona, wrote the company: "I have worn them [jeans] every day except Sunday since the early part of 1917. And for some reason which I wish you would explain, they have gone to pieces. . . . Please consider and let me know if the fault is mine." And Mrs. M. H. English of Otto, Wyoming, wrote in: "Going between here and Basin, we found a man who had run his car off the highway and was stuck. Had no chains or rope . . . but found a pair of old Levi's in the back of the car and tied one leg to our car and one to the front of his. We really had to pull, but the pants held and he came out." Ed Cray, in his book *Levi's*, comments on this reputation: "The singleminded focus on durability was, by the end of the decade, unusual in American business. Only one other manufacturer had so capitalized on quality in its advertising, and Henry Ford's Model T had become a byword for reliability. In significant ways, the Double X denim paralleled the success of the earlier automobile. Durability bred customer loyalty, and, uniquely, an affection for the product that transcended mere serviceability."

The Depression hit Levi as hard as it hit most companies, particularly since the company's chief product was aimed at the workingman—who, as often as not, was now out looking for a job. But the Western movie was growing in popularity, and when stars like Gene Autry began appearing in Levi's, sales got a boost. In 1937 the company added to its pants and jackets what was to become the best-known insignia in clothing history: the folded red cotton ribbon stamped "Levi's" that is found, for example, stitched into a pocket on a pair of Levi jeans. (That little red loop has since been copied, bootlegged, and in Eastern Europe actually hijacked for black-market use.) Soon customers were asking for Levi's by name. World War II expanded the market—more workers than ever were wearing jeans—and in 1950 the company celebrated its one-hundredth anniversary with sales of $22 million. In the seventy-seven years since the jeans were introduced, Levi had sold a total of 95 million pairs of them.

What followed in the next two decades, however, made this modest story of corporate success pale by comparison. The beginnings of the boom came in the 1950s. Marlon Brando turned up in jeans in *The Wild Ones*. So did James Dean in *Rebel Without a Cause*, and neither movie was a Western. Soon jeans had become a symbol of rebellion among the young, invaluably stamped with the seal of adult disapproval when public schools in many areas banned them. And as marketers were rapidly discovering, the young of the baby-boom generation represented an unusual amount of buying power. From a low of 2.3 million babies born in 1933, the number of births had risen to 3.8 million in 1947 and a whopping 4.3 million in 1957, the baby boom's peak. As the market itself expanded, so too did its taste for jeans.

By 1970 it would have been hard to find a boy, girl, man, or woman between the ages of five and thirty who had never worn a pair of jeans. Most owned at least one pair; some owned several. Social class and occupation made no difference. Neither did geography. Jeans sold well all over the United States; they sold well abroad. Like Coca-Cola, they became a pervasive symbol of America, worn both by those who wanted to ape American ways and by those who rejected—or thought they rejected—everything that smacked of Americanism. The adoption of jeans by young people all over the world was, as John Brooks put it in a *New Yorker* article on the subject, "an event without precedent in the history of human attire."

Levi wasn't the only company affected by this phenomenon. Blue Bell, a clothing manufacturer based in Greensboro, North Carolina, had decided to follow Levi into the jeans market shortly after World War II. Sales of the company's Wrangler line skyrocketed in the years that followed. But the effect on Levi may have been the most dramatic: it was, as Moskowitz and his colleagues put it, "like being kicked in the rear by a mule." The "private company that had been quietly making the garment for a hundred years . . . found themselves catapulted into the ranks of multinational corporations." By the end of the 1960s the company was selling tens of millions of pairs of pants and doing business worth hundreds of millions of dollars every year.

Why, with such a record, would any company be worrying about making new products? Part of the answer, obviously, is the sheer riskiness of depending so heavily on a single item. The boom in jeans was in many ways a historical accident, and what history has given it can also take away. A shift in taste to chinos or corduroys in 1970 wouldn't have left Levi high and dry, but it wouldn't have done the firm any good either. Without jeans, Levi Strauss would be just another big clothing company scrambling for markets.

Then, too, the demographics of the marketplace were already beginning to change. Jeans, to be sure, were no longer the exclusive province of youth: baby boomers who had grown up on Levi's kept on wearing them into their twenties. But they would no longer be wearing them everywhere and all the time, as they did when they were teen-agers. And the next generation of adolescents wasn't so numerous. The birthrate had peaked in 1957; by 1964, demographers agreed, the baby boom was over. The bulge in the population that the boom had created would soon be moving into a world of casual slacks, leisure suits, and coats and ties. From a marketing point of view, that's where the action soon would be.

Finally, the competition had been gearing up. Levi's had always shared the market with Blue Bell's Wranglers and other national brands like Lee. But now there were jeans all over. Back in 1970 Levi probably couldn't have foreseen the popularity of "designer" jeans skimming off the upper end of the market. But they could certainly anticipate cut-rate models gnawing away at the low end. To sell their wares, Levi knew, retailers would have to slash prices. The profit outlook in a saturated, competitive marketplace like this was bleak.

Faced with such a situation, Levi could have bought up another clothing manufacturer—though probably not one that made a lot of jeans, unless it wanted to run the risk of an antitrust suit. It could have bought up a company or two in another area entirely, thereby setting its corporate sights on the goal of becoming yet another conglomerate. Or it could choose to expand its own line, capitalizing on its expertise in making clothes, its reputation, its sales network, and its financial clout. The variables that affect this kind of decision can't always be measured. Risk assessments and profit potentials enter the picture, of course, but a lot depends both on the peculiarities of particular industries and on a company's managerial style. Unlike a specialty firm like Inforex (see Chapter Nine), Levi didn't have to worry that a technological breakthrough might render its whole product line obsolete. Jeans might one day falter, but clothing would always be good business. Also, Levi had always been a family-run firm, liberal in social matters but cautious in its business dealings. It had never sold stock publicly, and for sixty-eight years it occupied the same six-story yellow-brick building on San Francisco's Battery Street. The go-go style of the budding conglomerate did not seem to fit Levi Strauss.

For the Haas family that ran Levi, the solution was plain. In 1969 the decision was made to expand the company's line of products. In 1971 the firm "went public," selling over a million shares of stock at $47 a share. That provided money for further expansion. "In order for a company like Levi Strauss to extend its sales and profit growth"—as Peter Haas would put it later—"we need to diversify, to develop new products." Yet the pitfalls were plain too. "That," said Peter Haas, "is a lot more difficult than it was when we were just filling demand for a five-pocket western jean."

No PRODUCT retains its markets forever. Patents expire, competitors catch up, technology renders old products obsolete. For this reason no company can ever sit back and relax. Xerox, for example, dominated the plain-paper copier market for many years. Eventually competitors began to nibble away at the giant, sometimes offering comparable quality at a lower price, and Xerox scrambled to set itself up in other office-products markets. Polaroid saw its monopoly on instant cameras undercut by Kodak in 1976; it is now worried that the Japanese giant Fuji, which introduced its own model in Japan not long ago, has its eye on the United States. As a result it has moved into industrial and technological specialty markets for its cameras and film and has begun to experiment with new products such as batteries. Kodak itself doesn't sit still. The big camera company has challenged Xerox in copiers and Polaroid in instant cameras, and in early 1982 introduced a new snapshot camera (using film on a disc rather than on a roll) that it hopes will eventually displace the other snapshot cameras on the market. Nearly all those cameras, of course, are also made by Kodak.

The attempt to develop new products, though, is fraught with dangers. Xerox spent most of a billion dollars trying to take on IBM in the computer manufacturing business before retiring in 1975 in favor of word processors and other computer applications for the office. Polaroid had its Polavision, the $68-million instant-movie flop introduced in 1977 and retired in 1979. Of the two videodisc systems now on the market—the so-called CED system sold mainly by RCA and the laser-optical system sold by Pioneer and others—one, maybe both, will before long turn out to be a big loser.

Of the many cautionary tales of new product development, few are so likely to give a marketer shudders as the story of the Edsel. Cars and clothing, to be sure, are worlds apart. But Levi Strauss and Ford Motor Company aren't as different as they might seem. In both cases one man built up the company and passed it on to his heirs, who continued to run it. In both cases the initial products, as Cray notes, built their reputations on simplicity and durability. And in both cases the company name was solidly identified with the inexpensive, everyday-buyer end of the market.

In 1948 Ford saw the market changing, just as Levi did twenty years later. A marketing study that year revealed that families breaking into the $5,000-a-year income bracket—a relatively high bracket in those years, when the average manufacturing worker's wage was $1.33 an hour—traded in their old car for a more expensive model. The trade-up, however, was almost always to one of Ford's rivals. Later a Ford planning committee report projected the number of cars on the road at 70 million by 1965. "Half those American families earning $5,000 a year," the report said, "would buy medium-priced cars." Of the 2,900 new car models introduced since 1905, only 20 had survived. Nevertheless, Ford decided to build a new car. It would be targeted, the company said, "at the young executive or professional family on its way up." Ford asked poet Marianne Moore to come up with a name. Her choices—Intelligent Bullet, Utopian Turtletop, Pastelogram—lacked the ring of Detroit and Madison Avenue. So, as it turned out, did Ford's. Dismissing its own 2,000-name research study and its ad agency's 6,000-name list, Ford decided the car would be named for Edsel Ford, son of Henry, the company's president until his untimely death in 1943.

In keeping with the high secrecy surrounding the "E-car," as it was known within the company, Ford mounted a teasing ad campaign. A 1957 ad in *Life* showed an indistinguishable blur of a car speeding down a country road. "The Edsel," the ad announced, "is on its way." Two weeks later another ad appeared, this one showing a car covered with a white sheet. The caption read, "A man in your town recently made a decision that will change his life." That decision, the ad explained, was to become an Edsel dealer. "Whoever wrote that ad," observes John Brooks, the *New Yorker* writer who has chronicled this story, "cannot have known how truly he spoke."

Then in August 1957 came a three-day test preview, costing Ford more than $90,000. As Brooks describes it, "Edsels ran over two-foot ramps on two wheels, bounded from higher ramps on all four wheels, were driven in crisscross patterns, grazing each other at 60 or 70 miles per hour." Some 250 automotive reporters watched, and 71 set out in brand-new Edsels for delivery to automobile showrooms near their homes. On September 3, the day before the Edsel was officially introduced to the public, cavalcades of Edsels made their way down local throughfares. An enthusiastic dealer in California rented a helicopter to display an Edsel sign over San Francisco Bay.

At first the reviews were mixed. The automotive press liked the car, though noting its failings. But the January 1958 issue of *Consumer Reports* panned it. "As a matter of simple fact," said the magazine's engineers, "combined with the car's tendency to shake like jelly, Edsel handling represents retrogression rather than progress." Worse, consumers began to notice problem after problem. Oil leaked out; the hoods didn't push up. "*Automotive News*," Brooks writes, "reported that in general the earliest Edsels suffered from poor paint, inferior sheet metal, and faulty accessories. . . . A former executive of the Edsel Division has estimated that only about half of the first Edsels really performed properly."

All the market research and all the fanfare, it seemed, had made no difference. Somehow Ford had designed, engineered, and sold a car that didn't work as well as it should have and that consumers couldn't be persuaded to buy. Ford had hoped to sell 200,000 Edsels the first year alone. Two years and two months after it was introduced, the car was discontinued. Slightly fewer than 110,000 had been sold. The loss, Brooks estimates, was $350 million.

Though clothing companies do not operate on the same scale as Ford, some of Levi Strauss's earliest experiments with diversification had something of the Edsel about them. In 1954, flushed with the success of the cotton twill pants it had introduced a few years earlier, Levi brought out a line of permanent press slacks. Within six months 5 out of every 100 pairs sold had been returned, and Levi had to admit it didn't have the right fabric for permanent press. Fifteen years later, as the company was planning its major expansion, it hit on a couple of equally dramatic flops. First was the denim bathing suit—which, when wet, weighed the wearer down to the point of imminent drowning. Next was a line of disposable sheets and towels. These, Levi discovered, were not high on the consumer's list of priorities. Unable to interest hotels in the product, the company was saved when the factory that made the sheets burned down. Levi absorbed the $250,000 loss.

Eventually Levi created six new divisions, ranging from jeans to accessories and including a sizable effort in women's sportswear, Levi's for Gals. The diversification worked. In the mid-1970s Levi's sales hit the billion-dollar mark, having taken 125 years to reach that milestone. Four years later sales hit $2 billion. In 1979 the company ranked 167th on *Fortune's* list of the 500 largest industrial corporations, and 20th in net profits. By 1980 it was up to 138th in size and 18th in profits. Between 1970 and 1980 Levi had grown an average of 23 percent a year. In 1979 alone it sold 143 million garments.

In menswear, though, all Levi products had been aimed at the middle of the market. The company had brought out a line of moderately dressy slacks and polyester leisure suits—the Action Slack and Action Suit—and was doing a brisk business with them. But that tempting upper end of the market remained untouched. "If we want to grow we're probably going to have to go to upper moderate price points," one Levi official explained, "and somewhat higher taste levels for our products." In short, more expensive clothes—like the Tailored Classic. If Levi could sell sport coats, dress slacks, and above all suits, a whole new market would open up. The Tailored Classic might make money all by itself. But even more important, it would get Levi into the business of producing fancier and costlier clothing. The consumer would come to think of it as a manufacturer of dress apparel as well as jeans. That, in turn, would allow Levi to spin off many more such lines in the future.

*   *   *

LEVI'S FIRST STEP was to take apart the men's clothing market and put it back together again. An eighteen-month, 2,000-interview survey of men's tastes and buying habits in clothes allowed Levi to profile five distinct segments of the market. The company assigned them numbers, though in no particular order.

Q3, as Tailored Classic marketing director Steve Goldstein explained it, was the part of the market Levi had drawn on most in the past. "The Q3 segment we call the utilitarian jeans customer," Goldsmith said. "This guy's our old familiar Levi's loyalist. He doesn't care much about clothes and he wears jeans for work and for play." Mostly young, mostly without great sums of money to spend, the Q3 shopper nevertheless accounted for 26 percent of the market in Levi's survey.

Q4s were mainly young too: "trendy casual" was Levi's description. "Basically your John Travolta type," said Goldstein, the Q4 shopper buys high-fashion brands and "loves to be noticed." "He may wear jeans to work, but he really comes to life after dark." The Q4 made up 19 percent of the market.

Q5 was a price shopper, buying his clothes at discount and department stores, wherever the bargains were best. And Q1 was the "mainstream traditionalist." Where Q5 would buy anything that was cheap, Q1 went in for polyester. Most Q1s were married, most preferred to shop with their wives, most were over forty-five, most were conservative, both in politics and in taste. And Levi was already doing a good business with them. The Q1 shopper "really is the heart of our Levi's Action Slack and Levi's Action Suit business," said Goldstein, "which at the moment makes up a good portion of all the sales of the menswear division."

What was left, after all these segments were weeded out and assigned to their niche, was the shopper Levi was looking for. Q2, the "classic independent," was the kind of man who pays attention to his clothes. His taste was traditional: "lapels never too wide and never too narrow," as Goldstein put it. He bought most of his clothes in specialty stores— "looking right is real important to him"—and he went shopping alone, without wife or girl friend. And he spent a lot of money. Only 21 percent of the market overall, he nevertheless bought nearly half of all the costly wool and wool-blended clothing on the market.

Step Two. In June of 1980 Peter Haas was put in charge of a new marketing division, created specifically to introduce a line of clothing for the Q2 shopper, more expensive and more formal than anything Levi had produced in the past. Haas was a scion of the family that had run Levi for generations; he was also a Harvard MBA. Goldstein, who was to be his partner on the project, had been with the company five years. Before that he had marketed everything from plastic welding equipment and liquid yogurt to cold capsules.

In August a garment industry veteran named Steve Schwartzbach was given the job of designing and overseeing production of the new line. Schwartzbach assembled samples from other manufacturers to serve as models for the prototype garments, made his modifications and drawings, and came up with a classically designed set of clothes. By December he would have his samples for approval from the factory. Selling the line would be the job of George McGoldrick, sales manager for the Tailored Classic, and the twelve sales people who worked for him. The advertising manager was Leslie Shulman. Plans called for a television commercial trumpeting the line, but the commercial itself would have to be carefully targeted. Past Levi ads featuring eighteen-year-olds corkscrewing through space in their Levi jeans wouldn't work. This one would have to emphasize casual elegance. And unlike a lot of advertising for men's clothing there would be no woman in the picture. "That would antagonize the guy," Goldstein observed. "He doesn't want to have somebody telling him that he looks good or he doesn't look good."

Haas, Goldstein, Schwartzbach, and Shulman were the group that had gathered behind the one-way mirror to watch one of Malcolm Baker's focus groups. The focus group was an important part of Levi's market research: it was designed to give the company a qualitative insight into consumer attitudes and behavior and thus to supplement the largely quantitative 2,000-interview survey. Over the next year and a half every division of Levi would conduct a similar segmentation study, and they would all include focus groups. Typically, according to a report in *The New York Times*, a focus group moderator would "gently guide the group's discussion," starting with general conversation and moving on to more specific questions. Attitudes about company products would be elicited; reasons for particular behavior patterns would be probed. "Most major companies don't make decisions on the basis of focus groups," one expert told the *Times*. "But if they did just quantitative research, they wouldn't have any idea of what questions to ask."

Now, in November, it was still several months

before the Tailored Classic would be in the stores, and the Levi team needed to know what to expect. "The basis of this discussion," team leader Baker told the group, "is a fairly new concept in men's clothing. This is a full line of traditionally styled men's suits, with slacks and blazers, made of a natural and blended fabric. The clothes are reasonably priced and they require no tailoring. What are your reactions to this?"

Immediately a stumbling block appeared. "There's a big difference between something you take off the rack and something that you can have a little something done to," one participant was saying. "You have them do a little tailoring on it and it looks terrific on you." Haas, watching, drew the obvious lesson: "If they are mass-produced, it's the last thing the buyer wants to be reminded of." Goldstein concurred, making a note to stress the idea that the suits were being sold as separates. "The top fits your top and the bottom fits your bottom," he remarked to Haas.

Then came the final rub. "This line of clothing," Baker told the group, "will be made by Levi. Do you feel that Levi would do that well?" The customers were dubious. "I think Levi, I think jeans," said one. "If they're making suits, I'd have to be convinced." Later Baker summarized the reaction. "We have people saying, 'Well, if I want a suit and I went to work and someone said to me, "Hey, that's a nice suit, Joe, whose suit is it?" and I said Levi, I would not feel comfortable.' "

"It has a lot do with image," Baker explained, "rather than the belief that Levi is not capable of making a suit that would function perfectly well. My recommendation is to lead with slacks and sport coats and let suits slipstream. With the Levi image as it currently is, with this segment, however positive, I think the image is still a little too casual." So a paradox emerged. If Levi could get the Q2 shopper near the Tailored Classic line, he would very likely want to buy it. But the label would be an obstacle. And the company couldn't do without the label. Part of the purpose, after all, was to expand the firm's image.

There was another problem too. Levi had to sell to department stores: smaller stores couldn't give the manufacturer the volume it needed. But the Q2 shopper did his buying in stores that specialized in men's clothing. Could he be persuaded to reroute his shopping? Even he, Levi hoped, must be feeling the pinch of recession. In the department store, though, there was competition. Haggar, the Dallas-based menswear company, put out a similar line of suits. Haggar's "Imperial Separates," Levi argued, was for a different kind of shopper: the man who wanted an occasional suit. But Haggar couldn't be dismissed lightly. They had been in business since 1926, and men's suits were not a new item for them. As he left Baker's focus group, Steve Goldstein admitted the truth. "We have only one shot at this market. Everything we do relative to it has to be right."

DECEMBER 15, 1980. The selling of the Tailored Classic began. Steve Schwartzbach presented the line to buyers from Weinstock's department stores. A problem: wholesale prices were higher than anticipated. Retail prices would have to follow suit, and buyers were reluctant to commit themselves to large orders. By January 1981 McGoldrick and his sales force were having an equally tough time elsewhere in the country. Pattern layout and cutting were beginning at Levi's plant in San Antonio, and Levi had to decide by February 1 whether to exercise an option with Burlington Mills for more fabric. For the moment, sales were slow. And the salespeople were getting discouraged. Two reps quit the line: they weren't selling enough to make their commissions.

January 29, 1981. The garment trade magazine the *Daily Record* announced that Levi was dropping its prices between 4 and 7 percent. McGoldrick moved. "The biggest department store in the United States is Bamberger's, which is part of the Macy operation," he explained later. "They, I knew, were going to pass us. And they are big. They were going to Dallas, Texas, to work with our competition and place orders. The day that Pete got authority to roll back the prices, I caught a 1:00 A.M. plane to Dallas, found these people in their hotel eating breakfast at seven in the morning, ten minutes before our competition sent the limousine to pick them up, and saved the day. I felt like the cavalry coming. But they flew right from Dallas to San Francisco and they gave us—it must have been three, four hundred thousand dollars' worth of goods."

By March 10 the first selling season was over. The Tailored Classic team flew to Los Angeles for the annual menswear trade show called Magic. This was a big occasion—an opportunity for manufacturers and retailers to get together to display new products, make deals, and celebrate sales successes. Haggar was one of the companies doing the celebrating: sales of its Imperial line had more than tripled in the past year. Levi, however, wasn't so happy. Despite the price rollback, they had achieved only 65 percent of their sales goals. And the goals themselves were not particularly ambitious.

Worse, the word had come down from on high. Bob Segal, Peter Haas's boss, was losing confidence in the Tailored Classic. He canceled the television commercial and put all research on hold. The company, according to reports, saw more profit potential in its new line of washable polyester suits. Returning from Magic, Haas and Goldstein fought to keep the Tailored Classic alive, and decided to confront the disparity between the company's name and the line's elegance head-on. The ad agency prepared an ad to run in *The New York Times Magazine* in September: a picture of a horse and an elegantly dressed man. The caption: "Levi's Tailored Classics. You expected rivets, perhaps."

So the selling of the Levi classic moved forward—but at a walk, not a gallop. Eventually the team that put it together dispersed. George McGoldrick, after sixteen years with Levi Strauss, resigned. Unhappy trying to sell more expensive clothing under the Levi name, he took a job as national sales manager with RPM, a New York pants manufacturer. Peter Haas was assigned to the office of Levi's chief operating officer, and Steve Schwartzbach took over responsibility for the Tailored Classic. Steve Goldstein, meanwhile, was spending considerable time marketing the washable polyester suit—a product he was every bit as enthusiastic about as he had been about the Tailored Classic. "See, I can get enthusiastic about anything," he explained cheerfully. "I can get enthusiastic about a cheeseburger."

WHEN JACOB DAVIS, the Nevada tailor, developed his riveted pocket, he found the new product relatively easy to sell. For Levi Strauss, too, the problem of product development was relatively simple. Strauss could experiment from week to week with new materials, styles, or kinds of clothing. If his customers liked what he had to offer, he could give them more. If they didn't, he could cut back on one line and try another. Experimentation of this sort—keeping the customer satisfied, as the traditional sales refrain has it—is the heart of the free enterprise system. From the restaurant that changes its menu to the television station that offers a new news show, businesses always cast around for the products they think will attract the biggest or best-paying clientele.

For a giant corporation like Levi or Ford, however, experimentation isn't so simple. For one thing, the product itself may be technologically complex and therefore costly to build. Creating the Edsel required thousands of hours of design and engineering work, extensive research and experimentation with prototypes, and finally an expensive tooling up of the production lines. Producing any other sophisticated machine requires a similar investment: it can take years and cost many millions of dollars. Then, too, a large corporation's products aren't adequately tested until they have been marketed on a mass scale. The issue for Levi and Ford wasn't whether a few men would wear the Tailored Classic or a few drivers choose the Edsel. Both companies needed hundreds of thousands of customers and wouldn't be successful with fewer. But were the customers there? That question couldn't be answered until the products were available everywhere, until advertising campaigns had introduced them to buyers, and until customers could get used to the idea of the new product and make their decisions. Again, getting the answer was costly, both in time and in money.

Since product development can be such a lengthy and expensive process, companies ordinarily pose themselves a series of questions every time they plan a new product. First, is the product wanted? What are the gaps in the marketplace, and what wants are not being satisfied by existing products? Sometimes the answer to this question is simple enough: technology will create a new market. If a company develops a new computer system that out-paces existing computers but costs little more, for instance, it can count on finding a ready market. More frequently, however, a firm has to identify an existing market segment it believes can be tapped, just as Levi did. Utilizing extensive market research, it pinpoints a particular group of customers, a particular need, and a particular combination of quality and price. All these together constitute the company's anticipated market niche.

Second, can the company produce what is needed? Presumably the firm is already doing what it does best, but success in one market doesn't guarantee success in another. One way to reduce the risk is to follow the conglomerate's strategy of diversification through acquisition: you simply buy up a company that's already successful with a different product line. But often that option isn't open, or if it is a company chooses not to follow it. The firm must then determine whether it has, or can develop, the technical expertise, the production capability, the marketing network, and the sales acumen necessary to develop the product and get it to the customer successfully.

Once a market niche has been identified and a

company's capability established, the firm must plan its attack. This, as the case of Levi and the Tailored Classic illustrates, is above all an exercise in coordination. Designers and engineers must do their jobs in time to get production going, yet they must wait long enough to take full advantage of the company's market research. Most of the sales effort must wait until the product is available for inspection, but not so long that prospective buyers lose their initial enthusiasm or decide to take their business elsewhere. Advertising has to be coordinated with sales, and with the retailers' eventual marketing schedule. The job of planning all this activity falls to the executive in charge of the new product—in Levi's case, Peter Haas. For the moment, that individual, though a salaried employee, is as much the entrepreneur as Levi Strauss himself.

Then, of course, comes the marketplace's verdict. Some products catch on or flop instantly; others take years before the final decision is in. Still others adapt to the marketplace's wishes, or presumed wishes, to the point where they are almost unrecognizable. The Edsel unmistakably failed. The Thunderbird, introduced by Ford only shortly before, caught on, but appeared as a true two-seater sports car for only a few years before it was transformed into a four-seat luxury model. The Mustang, introduced in the 1960s, was a whopping success.

Levi was content to leave the Tailored Classic on the market for a while and see how it did. And sales did in fact begin to pick up. Slacks and jackets tripled in volume after the first selling period, and even suits held their own. The company, of course, could afford to wait. It was juggling some $400 million worth of new products, including ski wear and backpacking equipment, some of which were bound to succeed. And it had a lot going for it anyway. "Levi has instant name recognition, strong ties with retailers, and the marketing talent to identify and go after basic, profitable product lines," said Brenda Gall, an industry analyst with Merrill Lynch. It could not, to be sure, count on instant success, and the biggest obstacle, ironically, was the company's trademark, the one thing that couldn't easily be changed. But its assets, in the long run, could easily outweigh its liabilities.

The company's most famous product, the jeans themselves, is enshrined in the Smithsonian. That won't guarantee permanent success: the Edsel, after all, is enshrined there too. But if jeans ever go the way of the starched collar or the top hat, Levi, like Ford, will need something else to sell on the marketplace. Maybe at that point the Tailored Classic will turn out to be just what everyone was looking for. If not, it's a safe bet that Levi will have something else on the drawing board—or on the rack.

ONCE A PRODUCT is developed, it has to be sold. The task conjures up images of Willy Loman making his rounds or of Madison Avenue hucksters dreaming up new jingles. But marketing is neither mundane nor trivial. It involves not only salesmanship of different kinds but distribution systems, consumer testing, pricing, packaging, and everything else that helps move goods from provider to consumer.

All told, marketing expenses account for about

half of every consumer dollar. The reason is plain: without thorough and effective marketing, products can't compete in an already-full marketplace. A 1979 Gallup Poll, for example, indicated that only 20 percent of food shoppers enter the supermarket with a grocery list. The shopper's decisions as to what to buy are therefore heavily dependent on the way products are marketed in the store. Shelf space, advertising, brand-name packaging, and promotional devices like coupons all play a critical role in determining a product's sales.

Marketing is rarely an easy job. In the next chapter, two radically different business cases illustrate the difficulties entrepreneurs can confront, yet illustrate at the same time the critical importance of a successful effort. In one, Kentucky Fried Chicken takes its well-known product to a brand-new and strange environment, Japan. In the other, two writers put together a "package deal" for a book and movie, then must face the problem of how to make their work stand out from the crowd. In both cases, a product aimed at a mass market has to be rigorously pretested, packaged, distributed, and promoted. In both cases the people involved in selling the item have to be inspired and their work coordinated. The relative success of these efforts is the chief factor determining whether the products in question will succeed or fail.

6. Marketing

ON OPPOSITE SIDES of the Pacific Ocean, two groups of people are working on selling their respective products.

In Japan, a young woman who spends half her time visiting Kentucky Fried Chicken's many restaurants there is training a group of KFC employees. Her subject: The exact way to take a customer's order. One employee plays the role of customer while another takes and fills the order.

Virtually every step brings a correction. First the young man taking the order forgets to repeat it to the packer behind him. Later, when the "customer" orders sweet corn and ice cream, the order-taker forgets to ask what flavor ice cream. "When the packer has to ask what flavor," the trainer reminds him, "that's already too late." As the lesson continues, each employee gets a turn. Each is drilled repeatedly on the correct procedures.

Meanwhile, in Los Angeles, two authors are about to address the convention of the American Booksellers Association. The convention has brought hundreds of publishers together with representatives from hundreds of bookstores. It is a time for hard sell, soft sell, and everything in between, and the authors are wondering how best to make their pitch.

"We've got about ten minutes, right?" one author asks his partner. "These are hard-boiled sons of bitches, these guys."

The partner agrees. "They're going to have been hammered to death from a lot of chaps speaking to them before us, so the question is how hard we should push . . ."

"This is crucial to us," worries the first writer. "This is where Doubleday will pick up maybe a hundred thousand orders. This doesn't mean we go in and do a soft sell. . . . We want them to say this book's different because—and bang, you tell them why."

"Marketing," writes Harry L. Hansen in his well-known text on the subject, "is the process of discovering and translating consumer needs and wants into product and service specifications, creating demands for these products and services, and then in turn expanding this demand." The American Marketing Association defines it rather more simply: "Marketing is the performance of business activities that direct the flow of goods and services from producer to consumer or user." Unspoken in these definitions, of course, is the fact that marketing's purpose is not only to get products into the hands of consumers but to get product A instead of product B into those hands. In their book *Contemporary*

Business Louis E. Boone and David L. Kurtz note the importance of marketing in the pickle business. Vlasic Foods, which now sells 25 percent of the pickles in the United States, had to overcome food-industry giants like Heinz and Del Monte to reach its current preeminent position. The authors quote company president Robert J. Vlasic's explanation of the firm's success: "Most of our competitors were manufacturing-oriented, generations of fine pickle makers and proud of it. We came in exactly the opposite, as marketers who manufactured [in order] to have something to sell."

The first step in marketing was described in the last chapter: targeting the buyers and developing a product designed to appeal to them. The potential market can be broad. Everyone who does laundry, for example, can be considered a possible customer for a new brand of detergent, though companies may focus their marketing efforts on buyers thought to be most typical (such as women in a certain age range). Or the market may be narrow. The trade press—magazines aimed at people in particular industries or occupations—has flourished by creating new publications aimed at smaller and smaller occupational groups. A new Boston-based publication called *Test & Measurement World*, for example, is written for "the engineer or manager responsible for selecting [electronics] test and measurement equipment." This is a market whose members could almost be counted, one by one.

One part of product strategy, as it is known, is the choice of brand name, packaging, and everything else that goes into a product's image. Brand names are a relatively recent invention. Until Nabisco began packaging its crackers in boxes under the trade name Uneeda, crackers were typically sold unmarked from big cracker barrels in grocery stores. Soap, similarly, used to be "sold in large, unlabeled, unwrapped slabs from which the retailer would cut whatever amount the customer desired, wrap it in brown paper, and hand it across the counter," as one account describes it. Procter & Gamble changed that practice when it introduced its packaged Ivory brand in 1879. From the consumer's point of view, Ivory was an improvement over conventional soap—white, "99 and 44/100% pure," of uniform size and quality. Uneeda biscuits were wrapped and packaged and therefore fresh and sanitary. Buyers could ask for both products by name and be sure of what they were getting. From the companies' perspective the introduction of a brand name meant that Nabisco's or Procter & Gamble's products could now be distinguished from those of other manufacturers, could be advertised, and could be sold at prices determined by management. All the these marketing advantages meant substantially higher profits.

The second element of marketing is the distribution network itself. A manufacturer can take its wares directly to consumers through door-to-door selling, much as Avon salespeople distribute that company's products. More commonly, manufacturers sell to wholesalers, who in turn sell to retailers. But the range of possibilities is broad. A supermarket manager, for example, will buy some of his or her inventory direct from warehouses owned by food manufacturers and processors. Other items will come from food brokers, who act as middlemen between manufacturer and retailer. Still others will be provided by "rack jobbers," delivery people for bakeries and other enterprises who take responsibility not only for providing the goods but for stacking them on the shelves. Sometimes the distribution network determines the product strategy, even the brand name. Sears, for example, sells most of its wares under its own "house" labels and brand names. It determines its own product mix, then orders goods accordingly from a variety of manufacturers.

Advertising, promotion, and pricing strategies are the other key elements of marketing. Advertising takes place through a variety of media—newspapers and magazines, radio and television, billboards—and offers a variety of messages. Some ads, such as cigarette and beer commercials, emphasize a product's image as much as its more direct qualities such as taste. Other ads spell out very specific ways in which a product differs from its competition, such as low price. Promotional strategies include everything from public relations activities such as Virginia Slims' sponsorship of the women's tennis tournament to marketing gimmicks like cents-off coupons. Pricing is a means through which a company can target its market. Though prices are always influenced by supply and demand, any firm can choose various pricing strategies. Nor is the goal always to sell more cheaply than the competition. On the contrary, a high price may indicate high quality, prestige, or elegance and thus appeal to a more affluent buyer than a low price.

No one of these elements exists in isolation. Rather, a marketing strategy ordinarily involves combining them in whatever way best maximizes sales and profits. Most often, too, a strategy is put into place, then modified according to what seems to work best and what the competition is doing. The booming new market in personal computers is a good place to watch the broad outlines of developing marketing strategies. Leaders in the personal-computer field like Apple and Tandy/Radio Shack trade on their well-known brand names and on the wide variety of packaged software (the instructions that enable a computer to do different things) that is available for each. New entries in the field—Commodore, for example, and Sinclair—try to compete by offering smaller, less powerful computers at prices much lower than the leaders'. The distribution network in personal computers is only now beginning to take shape. Some are sold primarily by mail or through electronics stores. Others are sold through new computer stores. Still others are sold by big retailers like Sears. The extent to which various companies rely on salespeople will reflect their distribution strategies, and their advertising and pricing strategies will reflect the particular segment of the market they are trying to cultivate.

No cursory survey, however, can do justice to the complexities of marketing. In any given case there are a thousand different elements that go into the successful development, distribution, and selling of a product. The experience of Kentucky Fried Chicken in Japan and of two best-selling authors is in some ways atypical, but the two cases illustrate how varied marketing can be. Not coincidentally they also illustrate how successful marketing leads to a successful business—and vice versa.

FAST FOOD in America dates back to the mid-1950s. In 1954, according to the almanac *Everybody's Business*, a salesman named Ray Kroc was peddling a soda-fountain device known as the Prince Castle Multi-Mixer, capable of making six milkshakes at once. A hamburger stand in San Bernardino, California, owned by Richard and Maurice McDonald ordered eight of them. "Ray Kroc showed up there one day," write Max Boas and Steve Chain in their book *Big Mac*, "after deciding that he wanted a firsthand look at an operation that found it necessary to make forty-eight milkshakes at the same time."

What he saw was a pair of golden arches and a stand that Kroc estimated was doing $250,000 worth of business a year. His interest was not so much in the stand itself, however, as in its franchise potential. The McDonald brothers, having sold six franchises already, were reluctant, but the fast-talking Kroc convinced them to give him the go-ahead. Six years and many franchises later, he bought out the McDonald brothers for $2.7 million.

The McDonald brothers' and Kroc's innovations were all in marketing. Hamburgers and french fries, after all, were already being widely sold. But nowhere else could you walk in, place your order, and fifty seconds later walk out with a meal. Nowhere else were prices as low as they were at McDonald's. And all the restaurants were virtually identical. A customer in Maine and a customer in Texas could both walk into McDonald's knowing exactly what to expect. To ensure uniformity, McDonald's set up a rigid set of specifications both as to product—the weight of a hamburger patty, for example—and procedures. In any McDonald's, *Everybody's Business* says, "the french fries will have been cooked within the past seven minutes, the hamburger in the last ten. What's more, the bathroom will be clean and the parking lot free of teenage troublemakers."

Kentucky Fried Chicken traces its roots back to

1930, when a forty-year old man named Harland Sanders opened up a restaurant and gas station in the little town of Corbin, Kentucky. Sanders's career till then had been spotty: he had worked as a blacksmith's helper, railroad fireman, and insurance salesman, then invested all his money in an acetylene-gas-lighting business, for farms. That enterprise went broke when Delco came out with a superior electric-light system. But the restaurant he set up next did well. In 1935 the governor of Kentucky made him an honorary "Kentucky Colonel," and in 1939 his establishment was listed in Duncan Hines's famous guide, *Adventures in Good Eating.*

In the mid-1950s the government built an interstate highway that bypassed Corbin. Sanders, at sixty-six, had to sell his operation. Only then did he decide to try franchising his secrets, notably his already well-known chicken recipe. His method was somewhat different from Kroc's. "Traveling through Indiana, Ohio, and Kentucky," says a company history, "he called on restaurant owners, cooking his chicken for them and their employees. If they liked it enough to add it to their menus, they agreed to pay the Colonel a few cents for every Kentucky Fried Chicken dinner they sold." Within five years the colonel had 400 franchises, within ten years more than 600, including one in England. In 1964, at age seventy-four, he sold out to John Y. Brown and a partner for $2 million. Brown, who is now governor of Kentucky, sold out in turn to Heublein, Inc., in 1971. The price this time around was $275 million.

Today KFC does more than $2 billion worth of business worldwide. Its 4,500 outlets in this country employ about 70,000 workers. Most are franchised— that is, owned by independent operators who buy a license from KFC, follow certain specified rules in preparing and selling the chicken, and return a specified portion of their gross sales to the parent company. About 1,000 KFC outlets can be found in other countries. Though the Original Recipe chicken, as it's known, is always the same, the "fixin's" vary from place to place. Australians get rotisserie chicken and peas, the English get "chips," or English french fries. Guam's KFC customers get Tabasco and soy sauces to spice up the red rice that's served with the chicken, and Middle Eastern diners get a salad called tabouli instead of cole slaw.

The prize market outside the United States, of course, is Japan. Japan is a rich, populous country of some 120 million, 90 percent of whom consider themselves middle class. It is thus the second largest consumer economy in the world, outranked only by the United States itself. The Japanese are well disposed toward Americans and their products; Western models and celebrities, for example, appear frequently in Japanese advertising. And some American companies have made substantial inroads. Pepsi and Coca-Cola, for instance, currently account for over half of Japan's soft-drink market. Kellogg's Corn Flakes is the top-selling breakfast cereal and Nabisco the favorite cracker.

Other companies, however, have encountered obstacles. The Japanese way of business is a unique approach to commerce that combines modern methods with centuries-old traditions, and the signals may be hard for Americans to read. A 1979 U.S. Department of Commerce report on business opportunities in Japan cautions, " 'Yes' to a Japanese may often mean, 'Yes, I understand what you said,' and not necessarily, 'Yes, I agree.' " By the same token, though, firm personal relationships can lead to good business relations. "Everything here is based on trust in business," a Kentucky Fried Chicken official explains. "A handshake is more important than a contract. The Japanese won't do business with you unless they know, trust, and admire you. If you sit down together . . . very often it's at the end of the party where a deal could be struck." Partly because of such unfamiliar customs, many American companies have put together joint-venture arrangements with Japanese firms. Others set up subsidiaries managed by Japanese nationals; still others, like Japan McDonald's, simply license local manufacture or sale of brand-name products.

Where the restaurant business was concerned, the opportunities seemed to outweigh the obstacles. Japan is the restaurant capital of the world, with one eating establishment for every 81 people. In recent years, with income rising and leisure time more plentiful, the industry has boomed. Fast food in particular has proved inordinately popular, growing by a factor of six in the last ten years. As a result companies like Pizza Hut, McDonald's, Wendy's International, and Dairy Queen are all vying for the Japanese diner's yen. In 1979 there were 1,110 fast-food operations in Tokyo alone. The Kamakura branch of McDonald's that year did the most business of any McDonald's in the world.

Kentucky Fried Chicken began its Japanese operation in 1970 with two test operations, one at Expo '70 in Osaka, the other in a Tokyo department store. The company had a good product to offer: chicken is popular in Japan anyway, and KFC's chicken tasted a little like *yakitori*, the broiled chicken on a stick that is one of Japan's most popular dishes.

Still, the experiments were successful beyond all expectations. The Expo outlet broke records: sales there hit $100,000 a month.

Shortly thereafter KFC set up a fifty-fifty joint venture with Mitsubishi, the giant Japanese trading company. Mitsubishi could guide KFC through the Japanese bureaucracy, making sure it complied with applicable laws and followed appropriate customs. It gave KFC access to well-developed sources of supply. And it had interests of its own. A year before, Mitsubishi had bought heavily into the chicken feed and farm business. Now it could sell its chickens to KFC, which would be only too delighted to have a reliable supply.

The man KFC brought in to head its operation was Loy Weston, then about forty, a former IBM executive lured away from his employer and sent to Japan. Weston quickly found an assistant in Shin Okuara. When Loy first came to Japan, Shin was working for a printing and paper company. Sensing an opportunity to do big business in the cardboard boxes KFC would need, he came to see Weston. Loy was so impressed with the young man that he persuaded him to join KFC. Shin is now executive vice-president and the company's chief operating officer. He is responsibile for hiring, store location, and a variety of other key tasks.

SINCE THE EARLY 1970s KFC has muscled its way into the number-one spot in Japanese fast food. It has spawned 324 Japanese stores, roughly half of which are owned by the company and half by local franchises. Its annual sales top $200 million. The Japanese have nicknamed KFC *tsuiteru kaisha*—"the lucky company." Its success, however, probably has less to do with luck than with good management and astute marketing.

One step in the marketing strategy is determining store location. Where a typical KFC outlet in the United States is free-standing—and thus built to the same size and specifications everywhere—the typical Japanese store is located in an existing building. Many are smaller than KFC's standard size. "What we do is design a store appropriate for Japan," explained Weston. "Every time we find a little space, we design a way to fit our store in. We shrink equipment, redesigning it, making it taller instead of longer." KFC's outlets may be only one-third the size of American prototypes, but they do twice the business, an average of $620,000 a year.

Because rent is high in Japan, sites have to be selected with particular care. To qualify for consideration a district must have at least 50,000 people using its train station every day. The number of people 15 minutes away by bus or by foot is computed, and the number of passersby per hour is multiplied by store frontage, to produce something called the location factor. Then all these figures are fed into a formula designed to estimate sales. A new outlet in Kamiuati, a merchant district in northeast Tokyo, will cost KFC $400,000 to set up and equip, plus an additional $2,800 a month in rent. But even in this lower-middle-class neighborhood, sales are expected to reach $85,000 a month.

As in other countries, KFC varied the menu to accommodate local tastes. "The Japanese aren't thrilled about mashed potatoes and gravy, which are common in both the United States and Australia," Weston said, "so we switched to french fries." When Japanese consumers found the cole slaw too sweet,

KFC cut the sugar in half. The company catered to Japanese preferences in other ways too. Smoked chicken, yogurt, and fish and chips, for example, all adorn KFC's Japanese menus.

Two devices—one dictated by Japanese custom, the other a brainchild of Weston's—marked KFC's on-site promotional strategy. Every restaurant in Japan displays models of the food it serves in glass display cases near the door. The samples, made from wax and silicon, are cast from actual pieces of food, and factories specializing in manufacturing the models can provide anything from sushi and shark-fin soup to spaghetti and meatballs. One such plant provided KFC with a 13-piece set of chicken for $85 each. Every store had to have one.

Every store also got a life-size statue of Colonel Sanders himself to put on the sidewalk outside the door. These were Weston's idea. "I was stumbling around a warehouse back in Louisville gathering up equipment to come to Japan," he said, "when I saw this dusty statue of Colonel Sanders back in the corner. I had no idea what it was for, and nobody else seemed to know either, but I bought it and brought it to Japan. My idea was that the streets are crowded here, and one of these in front of every store would prove it was the authentic Kentucky Fried Chicken." Respected brand names and authenticity are highly valued in Japan, and the move made KFC outlets instantly recognizable.

KFC In Japan spends $5 million a year on television commercials alone. The account is handled by another joint venture, this one between a Japanese firm and the McCann-Erickson agency. The theme chosen in one recent year was KFC's Americanism—a big seller in Japan—and ironically, its aristocratic elegance. In one commercial, a camera panned over the fireplace of an "old Kentucky home" and focused in on a loaf of rye bread, ostensibly baked by Colonel Sanders when he was a boy. The commercial concluded with shots of Americans eating chicken. Weston was uncomfortable at first: "Are you telling me that the Japanese people are going to believe that this seven-year-old guy made bread?" But the agency people convinced him, noting that the commercial had tested well before general audiences.

Another aspect of the company's marketing effort is its extensive training of employees. "In Japan, when you hire, you hire for life," Weston said. "We train extensively because we know the employee is going to be with us his entire life. If you ask a KFC employee who he works for, he won't say, 'I work for KFC,' he'll say, 'I belong to KFC.' " The philosophy is reflected in managerial practices. Every morning KFC employees all over Japan repeat the company pledge. When they started, they got nine days of basic operation training and four days of on-the-job training. Instructors like the young woman described earlier made sure that every employee greeted the customer in the same polite, rigidly prescribed way. The franchisees, who pay KFC a $10,000 licensing fee plus 4 percent of their yearly gross, are similarly imbued with company spirit, though in a more relaxed atmosphere. Every year they are invited to an elegant restaurant, at company expense, the night of the annual KFC convention. The $9,000 this event costs in considered an expense well worth it.

Before opening a restaurant, the Japanese pursue a well-established strategy of personal selling. Capitalizing on the social nature of much of Japanese businesses, KFC representatives pay calls on local merchants in the neighborhood around an outlet. The store's managers introduce themselves to the other businessmen, offering gifts of smoked chicken and discount coupons for opening day.

On a typical opening day, the franchise is festooned with wreaths from the same local merchants. The wreaths offer messages of good luck and at the same time advertise the sender's business. Businessmen who consider KFC a prime client—the owner of the wax-replica factory, for example—are in dutiful attendance for opening-day ceremonies. So too are the store's landlord and representatives from Mitsubishi. They watch as a Shinto priest delivers a seventh-century prayer asking the gods' help for the new business enterprise. Using the fast-food counter as an altar, the priest christens the store with traditional symbols of good luck: rice cakes, sake, and dried squid, something from the mountains, something from the sea, something from the rivers. The priest uses a branch of a sacred tree to call the gods and goddesses. Finally, in a tradition borrowed from the West, there is a tape-cutting ceremony. The restaurant is open.

When the store in Kamiuati was opened by this procedure, it was mobbed the next morning with housewives and small children eager for a taste of its fried chicken. At that rate, KFC officials felt, the sales target of $3,000 a day didn't seem unreasonable. There was, to be sure, competition, in the form of an outfit called Church's Texas Fried Chicken, located literally down the street. But KFC remained confident. "Every time a new [competitive] store opens, our people get very excited," said Weston. "They say, 'How can we beat them, how can we improve our quality and our service and our cleanliness and just overwhelm them?' "

Weston's results the year Kamiuati opened were not spectacular. He had to report to his co-owners at Mitsubishi that profit targets had been missed by nearly $4 million. But even that did not worry the Japanese. "So far you and your company have made good progress," the head of Mitsubishi told Weston. "I'm not concerned with small ups and downs."

Weston was relieved. "I think the Japanese business executive has an advantage because he can plan for a longer time," he said. "He can explain to his bankers that he's going to have eight down quarters while he's building market share, and there's a correlation between profitability and market share. But try that out on a securities analyst in the United States and they'll dump your stock tomorrow."

Beyond its marketing expertise KFC had one more asset apparently working for it: local superstition. "KFC's buildings are shaped like pagodas," Weston explains, "and our company colors are red and white, Japan's national colors that stand for happiness. And we usually try to open our new stores on one of the twelve lucky days in the Japanese calendar. Once, because three is a lucky number, we opened three stores on March third, the third day of the third month."

It may be scientific marketing, but business has boomed. Weston remembers arriving for the opening day of a new outlet only to find the franchise's door built in a different place from the usual. "It turned out," he recalled, "that the Chinese astrologer had told the owner's mother that unless we put the door where he suggested, the store would be unlucky.

"He may have been right. The store quickly became the highest-volume unit in Japan."

MARKETING TAKES a variety of forms, depending on the industry. Some businesses, such as supermarkets, know that shoppers have to come to them, and so focus their marketing efforts purely on beating the competition. Businesses that rely on discretionary spending have to try to snag consumers' interest as well as beat the competition. The difference can be seen in the publishing industry. Textbook and reference-book publishers, for the most part, can count on a well-established, well-defined market. A typical textbook is produced according to rigorous specifications, often by editors working directly for the publisher rather than by independent authors. The same is true of reference books like dictionaries, encyclopedias, and specialized handbooks. Marketing efforts focus on actually getting the books into the hands of the consumer. Hence the phenomenon of door-to-door encyclopedia selling (or supermarket specials that allow customers to buy encyclopedias one book at a time). Hence, too, the attention paid by textbook sales personnel to wooing school systems and college professors. Because the market is assured, their job is only to get their book chosen instead of somebody else's.

Where trade publishing is concerned, the need is somewhat different. "Trade" books are those sold primarily through bookstores and primarily for general information and entertainment. Rarely does anyone *have* to buy a trade book; like a record or a movie it is a discretionary purchase. The task of marketing therefore, is twofold. One problem is to stimulate customers' interest, attracting them into the store. The second is to make sure that, once in the store, they pick up the intended book and buy it.

Traditionally, publishing has been a relatively genteel industry, run to a certain extent by "book people" rather than business people. In theory, if not always in fact, a publisher's interest was in publishing books with literary merit as well as books that, good or not, simply promised to sell well. Undue amounts of advertising and promotion in this context were sometimes thought to be rather tacky, conduct unbecoming a literary enterprise. In recent years, of course, the industry has begun to change dramatically. Three developments in particular are worth noting.

First, most of the top ten trade publishers are now owned by conglomerates. Random House, which was bought by RCA in 1966, was sold in 1980 to Newhouse Publications. Simon & Schuster is owned by the Gulf & Western conglomerate, William Morrow by the Hearst interests, Little, Brown by Time, Inc., and G. P. Putnam's Sons by MCA. Among the biggest of the trade publishers, only Doubleday remains a privately held company. In such an environment the importance of the bottom line has grown. Publishers, like other "profit centers" of a big corporation, are expected to pull their weight.

Second, despite the many stories of publishing's demise, the commercial appetite for the written word has, if anything, grown. Television, movies, and mass-market paperbacks all need stories. This need leads them to the people who write trade books and creates the possibility of "package deals," arrangements for books combined with television specials or movies. "Far from putting and end to publishing," noted *Saturday Review* literary critic Walter Arnold in 1979, "television is devouring and thus promoting books in made-for-television movies, specials, and miniseries." A TV or movie tie-in, in turn, promises enormous publicity and thus enormous potential profits for publishers. "When the publishers know there is a television deal or a movie," said one TV producer, "it does a great deal for them psychologically. They can see all the money they spend for public relations going toward something."

Third, writers have begun to take advantage of the marketing opportunities in this fast-developing industry to carve out lucrative contracts for themselves. A key figure in this development is the new role played by the literary agent. In *The Blockbuster Complex*, a book about changes in the publishing industry, author Thomas Whiteside quotes Howard Kaminsky, president of Warner Brothers. "Book publishing has become an agent-dominated business," says Kaminsky. "Some of the more active of these agents are also lawyers, whose experience both in adversary negotiations and in contract law has made for a new force in the business. This new force is being used to put together blockbuster deals involving a kind of multi-conglomerate interplay of hardcover and mass-market paperback publishing with television and movie production—an interplay calculated and programmed for maximum effect and employing all available devices for promotion and merchandising."

The result of all these developments has been a never-ending search for the blockbuster, the multimedia "property" that makes millions for all concerned. A classic example may be Alex Haley's *Roots*. When Doubleday published the book in 1976, it was a huge commercial success. But when ABC broadcast its seven-part miniseries, sales shot up all over again, this time reaching 100,000 a week. A more carefully planned series of tie-ins was the film *Superman*, released by Warner Communications. The company, according to sociologist Walter Powell, "released not one but eight Superman-related 'non-books' as part of the tie-in."

In all these ventures marketing plays a critical role. "The film industry," says Powell, "manipulates movie endings before test audiences in search of the one that gets the right audience response. . . . Following their media partners, book publishers now pay more heed to the artwork for a book's cover and to the accompanying publicity campaign." Where publishing used to be a sort of scatter-shot industry, Powell observes, "today's approach more closely resembles a cannon, wherein much time, energy, and money goes into one big product that is expected to appeal to a huge audience and offer spin-off possibilities for other media."

GORDON THOMAS and Max Morgan-Witts, two former BBC producers turned writers, are in some ways prototypes of the modern best-selling author. The two have different personalities: Thomas is a workaholic, worrier, and hustler, while Morgan-Witts is quiet and diligent. Despite these differences they evidently work well together. Through 1977 their seven books had sold 24 million copies in 23 countries and had made the pair millionaires many times over.

In 1977, looking for a book idea, the writers talked with NBC producers Frank Levy and Mike Wise. The ideas ranged from the story of Mary Jo Kopechne's death at Chappaquiddick to the stock-market crash of 1929. To find out which would sell best, NBC polled representative viewers. The winner was the '29 crash.

First the authors and agent Jonathan Clowes negotiated a deal with Twentieth Century Fox and NBC for a television miniseries based on the book, later to be released abroad as a feature film. Fox and NBC shelled out a $100,000 advance. Thomas and Morgan-Witts then turned to publishers, first the British firm of Hamish Hamilton and then the American giant Doubleday, who put up advances totaling $300,000. With various sublicensing agreements, the authors' total came to better than half a million dollars—before one word had been written.

Contracts in hand and checks deposited, the authors retired to Thomas's tax-shelter estate in Ireland to work. Earlier they had worked out a deal with *Reader's Digest*. In return for serialization rights, the Digest provided the writers with boxes of research material—typewritten files, tape recordings, clippings, books, old photographs. To give their book faces, voices, and locales, the authors traveled all over the world, visiting 23 countries and interviewing 438 witnesses. Later, in writing the book, they would be careful to include some material about every country in which the book would be sold.

The writing itself began in early 1978, with December of that year as the deadline for completion. Dividing up chapters according to interest, Thomas and Morgan-Witts wrote as quickly as they could, then gave each chapter to the other one for editing. After seven books together, they had the system well mastered. Eighteen months after the idea was born, nine months before the September 1979 "pub date," and four days before deadline, they got the book finished. The title: *The Day the Bubble Burst: The Social History of the Wall Street Crash of 1929.*

One by one the reactions came in, and all were positive. NBC producer Levy announced that it was everything he and the network had hoped it would be. "We had one concern from the beginning of the project, that the writers would just cater to the wealthy and business people, and we were worried about whether people in Iowa really cared about how the rich lived in 1929. But they found a lot of average people, and I think that's going to make the picture come to life at the network." The publishers too were overjoyed. A Doubleday editor, Sandy Richardson, pronounced it "marvelous." Another editor, Christopher St. Clair Stevenson of Hamish Hamilton, said simply, "It's the best book of yours I've read. It really has all the earmarks of one of our major books."

Still the book would need to elbow its way onto the shelf and into the hands of readers. The job wouldn't be easy: an average of 82 new titles a day are produced in America, and Doubleday alone publishes a new title every 12 hours. Doubleday was banking on selling between 125,000 and 140,000 copies of *Bubble*, enough to put it well up on the best-seller list. And it was willing to spend between $75,000 and $100,000 in marketing it. But the prime job of selling it was up to the two authors. "I think we recognized a long time ago that this job has many facets," said Thomas. "There's the research, the writing, and the essential part—the promotion. We really have to get out there and sell it. That's part of our job."

First step: the booksellers' convention. There, with

most of the publishing industry in attendance, Doubleday could pick up big orders, particularly if chains like Waldenbooks and B. Dalton got interested. The writers' speech, planned in advance, went well. The next step was to get the word out to the book trade through all other available channels. Columnists at *Publishers Weekly*, the Washington *Star*, and *The New York Times* were contacted. Promotional material was mailed to 5,000 top Doubleday accounts and 1,000 publicity lists. The company's catalog featured a special ad for *Bubble* on its inside front cover. The only hitch in this period, which was still several months before the book's actual publication, was at NBC. Miniseries had gone out of fashion at the network, and Frank Levy was worried that the dates and time wouldn't work out.

Typically a book is shipped out to bookstores six weeks before its formal publication date. Reviews appear, by convention, on or after the publication date. A critical part of the marketing effort at this stage is the author's tour. Tours are arranged and interviews are set up by the publisher: the authors appear on talk shows, give interviews to newspaper journalists, autograph copies of their book at bookstores. The pace can be grueling. "Most author's tours nowadays last three to four weeks," wrote the *New York Times Book Review* columnist Ray Walters, "including stops in ten to fifteen cities, with scarcely a moment to rest. They may call for a half-dozen engagements a day. Through it all, the author must remain smiling, quick-witted and gussied up, undaunted by the travails of travel."

Doubleday sent Gordon Thomas on the Northern route: Chicago, Minneapolis, Seattle. Max Morgan-Witts started in Boston, then went the Southern route, hitting Washington and Atlanta, among others. Both ended up in Los Angeles for the network shows. The pace was everything it was cracked up to be. "We'll get up at five," explained Thomas, "and do an early-morning breakfast show. That's the first, but before eight o'clock we'll probably have done three. Between eight and nine we'll do newspaper interviews, and then we'll do another mid-morning TV show. Then we'll jump on a plane at eleven and fly a thousand miles, and repeat. Our days will be sixteen or seventeen hours long."

IN OCTOBER 1979 *Bubble* hit the best-seller list. But it didn't last long. A review by Geoffrey Barraclough in *The New York Times Book Review* lumped it together with two other books and gave it only a lukewarm recommendation. All told, the book sold only 45,000 copies in hardback, about one-third of Doubleday's projections. The TV movie, meanwhile, was repeatedly postponed. This meant that Penguin, which had bought the paperback rights, had to bring out the book without benefit of the television tie-in. When the movie was finally aired—on February 7, 1982—it bombed in the ratings.

Ironically the package was still a financial success for many of the participants. Doubleday didn't sell as many hardbacks as it wanted, but it did sell the paperback rights to Penguin for a fat sum. Every time the movie was rescheduled, NBC cranked up its own promotional machinery and thus boosted Penguin's paperback sales. The authors, of course, probably did best of all, primarily because they had negotiated such lucrative arrangements in advance. And their book's performance didn't particularly hurt them. On the contrary, their own performance as marketers won them a good deal of respect and admiration in the industry. Shortly after *Bubble*, in fact, they went to work on their next book—a "medical detective story" about Legionnaire's disease, published in 1982. That too was sold as a package deal.

HOW IMPORTANT is marketing? Every firm obviously needs some system of getting its goods from the production lines into consumers' hands, and of making sure that potential customers know what it has to offer. In this sense marketing is a necessity. But the relative importance of various marketing techniques varies widely from industry to industry.

In general, marketing grows in importance as an industry matures and the possibility of technical advance declines. Henry Ford's Model T was demonstrably cheaper and more durable than most of its competitors, and for years Ford's chief marketing concern was only to make sure cars found their way into buyers' hands. His disdain, at the time, for the finer points of marketing was reflected in his famous dictum that customers could buy any color Model T they wanted, so long as it was black. When competitors like GM caught up with Ford technologically, though, matters like color and styling grew in importance.

A similar shift can be seen in parts of the computer industry today. The minicomputer business, for instance, includes two sizable Massachusetts-based companies, Digital Equipment Corporation and Data General Corporation. Data General in particular was notorious for its lack of concern with marketing: as a report in *The New York Times* put it, the firm had "built a reputation as a feisty, hard-charging computer company where engineering was a passion and marketing an afterthought." Yet it grew rapidly, mostly by selling its equipment to companies known in the trade as original equipment manufacturers, or OEMs. The OEMs bought hardware from Data General or its competitors, added appropriate peripheral equipment and software, and sold the complete system to buyers.

Over time, however, the buyers grew more sophisticated about computers and sought to bypass the OEMs, buying their equipment direct from the manufacturer. That meant the manufacturers had to deal with a larger, more varied group of customers— and that they had to pay more attention to marketing their wares. Digital Equipment, according to *The New York Times*, "responded quickly with a large sales and service organization." But Data General was slow to follow Digital's lead. Earnings, consequently, suffered.

The story illustrates a second general principle as well: marketing varies in importance with the degree of competition a company faces. The only restaurant in a small town, or the only newspaper in a big one, can afford a relaxed marketing strategy. A company faced with direct competition for its market, by contrast, ordinarily has to adopt an aggressive strategy. The importance of marketing can be seen most clearly in mature industries dominated by a few large firms, each of which produces a similar line of products and each of which is jockeying for market share. Breakfast cereals, cigarettes, beer, tires, and airline travel are all industries that fall into this category. So too, of course, are soaps and personal-care products—one reason why Procter & Gamble is the nation's largest television advertiser.

Lastly, marketing's role in a company's operations depends on its contribution to the firm's profitability. This principle, which is obvious enough, helps to explain some apparent anomalies of the business world. In most cities, for example, the telephone company's *Yellow Pages* is a unique product, enjoying a monopoly over its particular form of comprehensive classified advertising. Yet the phone company typically employs a large staff to sell ads in the Yellow Pages and periodically urges television viewers to "run your business big in the Yellow." It does so, of course, because the product is for practical purposes infinitely expandable: the more ads sold, the more money there is to be made. Not all enterprises find themselves in such a situation. A doctor with a full practice, a restaurant that has to turn away diners, and a factory operating up to capacity don't have a similar incentive to expand, and the role of marketing in their affairs will be correspondingly smaller. Similarly, if a firm has other avenues to increased profits—developing a new product, cutting its costs, or reorganizing production, for instance—it may choose to focus on these and let marketing take a back seat.

Where Kentucky Fried Chicken was concerned, the "technological advance" represented by fast-food restaurants had already been accomplished. Loy Weston's job was not to introduce fast food to Japan but to ensure that as many customers as possible chose KFC over Church's or indeed over McDonald's. The competition was stiff, and success depended both on developing a reputation and on making the product conveniently available to would-be diners. The more time and money he spent on expansion and advertising, the more profitable the enterprise would be. Marketing thus occupied a prime position in his list of priorities.

Gordon Thomas and Max Morgan-Witts, though their "product" was quite different from Weston's, were in a similar position. Their work would not, presumably, be classified as great literature. Nor was it a book that any group of people particularly had to buy. Rather, readers had to be introduced to the product, reminded of it as frequently as possible, and persuaded to buy it rather than some other book. Again, marketing was the chief means by which *Bubble* could be set apart from the competition.

There is, to be sure, a limit to what marketing can accomplish in any situation. Diners will not patronize a restaurant that serves unappetizing food, and readers will not buy a book their friends tell them is boring or uninformative. Then, too, there are some situations, as noted above, when marketing is relatively unimportant. The first person who builds the proverbial better mousetrap has only to make customers aware of the invention, then sit back and wait for orders.

In the middle, though—which is to say where most businesses find themselves—astute marketing can make the difference between success and failure. Most products, after all, are useful, of reasonable price and quality, something that people will want to buy. Making sure that this potential demand is translated into sales is the job of the marketer.

THERE ARE TIMES, one suspects, when those who run a business would dearly love to wish their competitors out of existence. If Levi didn't have to worry about Haggar, if Loy Weston didn't have those other chicken vendors down the street, how much easier life would be. The problems of finance, product development, and marketing could be taken on one at a time, almost at leisure, without that gnawing worry that someone else might be beating you to the punch.

Competition, of course, is a fact of life. Even businesses that enjoy a seeming monopoly have to take into account the consumer's alternatives. A town may have only one newspaper, but its residents can choose to watch the news on television instead. A gas utility has to be sure its prices are low enough to keep homeowners from switching to oil. Even the phone company, as we will see in Chapter Ten, has had a raft of competitors nibbling at its heels in the last several years.

Yet, though competition itself is nearly universal, businesses can choose to compete in a variety of ways. A company can go head-to-head with its competitors, matching them product for product and price for price. Or it may decide to carve out its own market niche, offering a particular product or service that is just a little different from everyone else's. The range of possible strategies is broad, and a lot usually rides on the outcome. So a business's approach to its competition can make a fascinating story.

The next chapter tells two such stories. In both

cases a big company's future is potentially at stake. In both cases, too, the competitors make crucial choices about how to take on their adversaries. The lessons to be drawn from these examples are not simple, for there are no easy solutions to the problem of competitive strategy. But they illustrate a fundamental point that is simple enough. In business it's not enough to make a good product and sell it at a reasonable price. You also have to be prepared to slug it out with those who say they're offering something better, cheaper, or both.

7. Competition

A MODERN jet airliner is an impressive machine. The largest can carry up to 500 people; the fastest can top 600 miles per hour. It is also expensive, for all concerned. To develop and build a new jet costs so much that a manufacturer must sell at least 500 just to break even. To buy one costs an airline up to $50 million, and to keep it in the air costs thousands of dollars a day more just for fuel and personnel. All these bills have to be paid, ultimately, by the air traveler—whose flights are subject to the vagaries of weather, airport delays, the economy, and personal whim. Making money by making or flying commercial airplanes is not the easiest thing in the world.

Not so long ago, both Boeing Aircraft and Eastern Airlines offered eloquent testimony to this fact. In the late 1960s Boeing was banking on two new projects. One was the 747 jumbo jet; the other was

161

the supersonic transport (SST). Congress killed the SST on the grounds of its potentially adverse environmental impact. Economics, it seemed, was killing the 747. Not until 1972 did the manufacturer get a single order for the plane. Thornton Wilson, then president of Boeing, slashed the company's work force from 105,000 to 38,000. In Seattle, where Boeing is headquartered, the unemployment rate rose to 13 percent, and a billboard appeared asking, "Will the last one to leave Seattle please turn off the lights." Eastern, meanwhile, was running into troubles of its own. Burdened with debt and hit hard by a slumping economy, the company lost $57 million in 1973. By 1975 it was losing $96 million and was close to collapse.

In the years that followed, both companies managed a dramatic turnaround. Eastern signed on former astronaut Frank Borman as president in 1975. Borman thinned the ranks, sold off some of the airline's old planes, and got employees to accept a deal whereby 3.5 percent of their wages were withheld, to be paid out only if the company made money. Helped by the recovering economy, the company turned a tidy profit in Borman's first few years. Boeing began making money too. Sales of the 747 picked up, and Boeing's earlier 727 model turned out to be the most successful jetliner ever built. In 1980 *Time* magazine put Thornton Wilson on its cover and announced that the company "dominates world aviation."

As the decade drew to a close, though, both Boeing and Eastern had a surprise awaiting them. Both were big, successful companies with well-established positions in their industries, yet both suddenly found themselves facing a feisty new competitor eager to knock them out of that position. And in each case the competitor had a potentially dramatic advantage. The result was a couple of knock-down, drag-out economic battles in which the giants, if not bowed, were at least bloodied.

TO A BYSTANDER, economic competition ordinarily appears in one of two guises.

In one guise competition resembles a basketball game, where the competitors all know the rules and try to outdo each other within a carefully defined set of limits. Miller competes with Budweiser—or Procter & Gamble with Colgate-Palmolive—essentially through advertising, through marketing gimmicks, and through jockeying for an occasional edge with a new or newly packaged product (Lite beer, Crest gel). Low price is rarely an issue, except during a "cents off" promotion campaign. Most of the products bear a striking resemblance to one another, and most are expected to share the market with their competition. The struggle is over how large each one's share of the market will be.

The paradigm of this sort of competition is, of course, cigarettes. Nearly all brands cost the same; nearly all in a given category (filtered, unfiltered, low-tar, menthol, etc.) are virtually indistinguishable. For this reason the ads rarely play up the particular attributes of any one brand. Instead they trumpet the brand's general qualities (great taste!) and subtly create an "image" to go along with it. The man who buys Marlboros or the woman who buys Virginia Slims is buying that image as much as he or she is buying a pack of cigarettes. The companies spend millions of dollars a year trying to increase their market share by this means.

Competition's other guise resembles more a boxing match than a basketball game. Instead of trying simply to outscore opponents, a competitor tries to knock them out. In business terms the objective is not to jockey for market share but to corner the market. There are, to be sure, rules and regulations that must be obeyed, just as in boxing. But within those rules anything goes. The popular name for this kind of competition—cutthroat—suggests what's at stake.

Cutthroat competition shows up in a variety of contexts. Americans old enough to drive before 1973 may remember "price wars" among gas stations. One station advertised a lower price than that offered by its competitor across the street. Soon the competitor lowered its price, the first one went still lower, and so on. Eventually both stations would wind up selling at a loss—and if the price war continued, the one with the least financial backing had to go out of business.

Interestingly, it was exactly this sort of competition that characterized the first big businesses in America, the railroads. "Never before," writes the historian Alfred D. Chandler, Jr., in his book *The Visible Hand*, "had a very small number of very large enterprises competed for the same business." And never before had competition been potentially so ruinous. Because each railroad was saddled with high fixed costs—for track, rolling stock, and the like—all were constantly tempted to cut rates in order to get more business. And when one cut, others had to follow suit, even if the new rates were too low to make a profit. "The logic of such competition," Chandler observes, "appeared to be bankruptcy for all."

To head off cutthroat competition of this sort, the railroads pursued a variety of strategies for divvying up the marketplace. Their efforts met only partial success, until the 1887 passage of the Interstate Commerce Act set up an agency to regulate rates and routes. Other big companies at the time, of course, were eliminating the competition by other means. Some simply undersold smaller competitors until the smaller were driven out of business. Others set up holding companies and trusts to buy up all the competitors in an industry and fix the industry's prices. Eventually the Sherman Antitrust Act regulated some of the more egregious of these "competitive" practices. But the whole episode illustrates the fundamental paradox of cutthroat competition. If a competitor is too successful, everyone else will be driven out of business and the winner will have the field to himself. At the same time, if a few of the competitors are successful and grow strong, no one will be able to do in the others. At that point cutthroat competition disappears and market-share competition takes its place.

Businesses rarely choose what kind of competition to engage in. That is determined for them—by laws and regulations, by the structure of their industry, by their own financial situation, in some cases by technology. What businesses do have to do is choose a competitive strategy. This, in turn, involves looking at three variables.

1. *Product and market niche.* What, exactly, is the competition offering? Goods and services are seldom exactly alike; even a gas station can sell its mechanics' skill or its willingness to wash windshields along with its gasoline. And rarely is every

possible niche in a marketplace occupied. Perhaps there's a need for a specialty product, or for a product that's much like the competition's but a little cheaper. Perhaps there's a need for a product that lasts longer, as evidenced, for example, by a warranty. Price, quality, and a product or service's special attributes all go into defining its market niche. Companies can try to elbow a competitor's product out of a market niche where it appears vulnerable, or they can try to create a product that fills an empty niche.

2. *Marketing.* As this book has discussed, marketing includes a variety of efforts: advertising and promotion, a distribution network, and any other means by which a firm gets it wares onto the shelves and into consumers' hands. Sometimes a company can compete through marketing alone. It can mount a new ad campaign, add to its sales force, or simply find a more efficient way to peddle its goods. The business of selling books, for example, has been revolutionized in recent years by the rise of stores such as the Waldenbooks and B. Dalton chains. Like supermarkets, these stores are driving a number of smaller operations out of business and are doing so primarily because they can get certain kinds of books into consumers' hands more effectively and more cheaply. Their size gives them clout with publishers. It also gives them the ability to advertise heavily and to offer discounts to consumers.

3. *Timing and context.* Like runners in a long-distance race, companies have to decide when to make their move. Sometimes a competitive move is brought on by internal changes, as when Philip Morris bought the Miller Brewing Company and decided to challenge Budweiser for national leadership

in beer. Other times it is touched off by external events such as a new technological development or a shift in consumer preferences. The OPEC-induced rise in oil prices, for instance, set the auto companies scurrying to see who could produce more fuel-efficient cars.

Like most business concepts, competition is best understood not in the abstract but in the concrete. For though the variables can be studied and measured, they do not obey the laws of physics. Competition in the end is a human interaction, involving a variety of opportunities and problems that those who run a business must face up to or take advantage of. In this context the stories of Boeing and Eastern are useful case studies. Both the airframe industry and the airline industry are well acquainted with the shifting sands of competition. Both stories illustrate how a challenger can take on even a well-established competitor, how the giant can react, and how market-share competition can sometimes turn cutthroat.

THE AIRFRAME INDUSTRY, as the companies that design, build, and market aircraft are known, is dominated by three giants. Boeing, Lockheed, and McDonnell-Douglas all have their roots in the World War I era, and all have pursued similar goals. Yet their relative success has shifted markedly over time.

William Edward Boeing started his business in Seattle, building his first stick-and-wire seaplane in just six months. The Loughead brothers (who later changed the spelling of their name) set up shop in Santa Barbara in 1916, the same year as Boeing. Donald Wills Douglas didn't start his own company until 1920 and didn't get an airplane produced until two years later. In 1924, though, two of Douglas's World Cruiser planes made the first trip around the world. The journey took six months and six days.

Douglas got off to a fast start in commercial planes, building the Douglas Commercial (DC) series that peaked first with the DC-3. The DC-3, with more than 13,000 produced, remains the most successful commercial airliner ever built. Boeing produced the Stratoliner and the famous Clipper flying boats used by Pan Am. After World War II the competition heated up. Building on its success with big, durable bombers like the B-17 and B-29, Boeing came out with the 377 Stratocruiser, a giant two-deck transport used by Northwest Orient Airlines. Lockheed produced the Constellation, and Douglas continued with its DC series through the DC-7. The latter, brought out in 1953, was the first commercial plane to fly across the country nonstop.

At this point Douglas was solidly in the lead. Lockheed's Constellation was second, and Boeing was a poor third, with only 56 Stratocruisers sold. The advent of the jetliner, though, reversed these positions. Now Boeing was first off the mark. A prototype of its 707 appeared in 1954, and American Airlines immediately placed an order. Five years later American flew the first scheduled jetliner flight, traveling from Los Angeles to New York in just over four hours.

Douglas never quite caught up. Its DC-8—like the 707 a narrow, sweptwing, four-engine plane with three seats on either side of the aisle—was successful but late. Worse, the company never wholly solved its production problems with the DC-8. By 1966 it was losing money and was ripe for a takeover; a year later it found a savior in James McDonnell of

McDonnell Aircraft in St. Louis, and McDonnell-Douglas was born. Lockheed, meanwhile, had failed miserably with its prop-jet Electra and was relegated for the time being to the military market. So Boeing and McDonnell-Douglas continued their competition through another generation, Boeing with the three-engine 727 and the smaller 737, McDonnell-Douglas with the DC-9. The 727, the world's best-selling jetliner, sold 1,500. The DC-9, also successful, sold over 900.

The next wave of innovations brought another flip-flop. This time Boeing apparently guessed wrong. Its new 747 jumbo jet, airlines felt, was too big. The SST was always a dubious prospect, and few outside the industry shed a tear when Congress finally killed it. McDonnell-Douglas, however, seemed right on the money. Its new DC-10, wide-bodied but not as big as the 747, offered just the flexibility that the market needed. And Lockheed, after sticking with military planes, ventured again into the commercial market with the L-1011 TriStar. Both planes were a third smaller than the 747 and could fly only half as far, but they only cost two-thirds as much. In the early 1970s they seemed big enough, and Boeing was out in the cold.

Slowly, though, this ranking too rearranged itself. The 747 caught on and Boeing's 727 continued to be a big seller. The DC-10 peaked in sales in 1975, only to be all but finished off later by a series of accidents including the 1979 Chicago crash that killed 275 people. Lockheed, meanwhile, almost went broke. Cost overruns on its military C5A cargo plane came to $2 billion, and the government balked at making up the difference. The engines for the TriStar were supposed to be coming from Rolls-Royce, just as Rolls-Royce was itself nearly giving up the ghost. A 1971 loan guarantee from the government squeaked by the Senate—and kept Lockheed alive long enough for a 1975 scandal involving questionable payments to Japanese officials to hit the headlines. As the 1970s came to an end, Boeing sat on top of the heap. Its patience, and the mistakes of its competitors, had finally paid off.

BY 1978, HOWEVER, it was clear that the 747 was never going to be the big seller Boeing had once hoped it would be. It was also clear—from the airframe industry's leapfrog history if from nothing else—that Boeing couldn't sit back and relax. McDonnell-Douglas's DC-9s were aging, but so were Boeing's 707s and 727s. Now the challenge to the industry was to come up with a quieter, highly fuel-efficient plane that could carry about 200 passengers. That size would put it midway between the 727/DC-9 class and the larger DC-10s and L-1011s. An airframe company planning to develop such a plane would have to be prepared to spend hundreds of millions of dollars on designing and building it. And none would start construction until it had a firm order from an airline—a launch order, as it is known—in hand.

Each of the companies had three choices. It could do nothing, coasting along with existing products. It could modify its existing line to meet the market's new needs. Or it could start from scratch with a "clean paper" design and build a brand-new plane. The first choice was no choice at all: to do nothing would be suicidal for any firm interested in maintaining a share of the commercial aviation market. But each of the other two choices had its advantages.

Modifying existing planes, of course, is cheaper. Major modifications of existing designs might cost between $100 and $200 million, while a clean-paper design could run between $1 and $2 billion. Of course, clean-paper designs might not succeed technically. The DC-10 is suspected of having design flaws in its retractable wing slats, which may have contributed to the crashes in which it was involved. A company could spend a billion dollars developing a new plane only to find it had some flaw that would be fatal to sales. Finally, a modified plane could be more or less counted to sell, simply because it had a record to build on. A new plane's sales potential couldn't be predicted. Moreover, most planes are either clear successes or clear failures. A new plane that turned out to be a flop could drag the company that produced it down as well.

On the other side of the ledger, a new plane by definition gives the designer a clean slate. Like a home builder who incorporates the latest in insulation or solar-heating technology, the designer can incorporate all the latest advances and can shape the plane around the customer's needs. To a company prepared to take the risks of a clean-paper design, the possibilities of matching a new plane to the changed market were tempting.

Lockheed and McDonnell-Douglas had no intention of starting from scratch. There were no new technological breakthroughs to apply to new planes, they argued. More important, they had models that would lend themselves to modification. Boeing was less well positioned in that respect. Its 747 was too big, its 727 too little, and its 707 too old and too skinny. If it didn't go to a clean-paper design, it would likely lose out to the derivatives of the DC-10 and the L-1011 the other companies would likely bring to market. But Boeing had an advantage the others didn't: a more favorable cash position. With $4 billion in its coffers, it could go for a new plane more easily than could either of its competitors.

So Boeing planned three new planes: the 767, which was the center-piece of its new line; the 777, a tri-jet version designed with American Airlines in mind; and the 757, which would have many components shared with the old 727. All would use a new "supercritical" wing design, new materials, and new engines. They would be much quieter and 35 percent cheaper to operate than the older planes. A launch order from United Airlines in July 1978 gave Boeing the final commitment it needed. United wanted 30 each of the 767 and the 727-200, a new version of that plane. With the new models, Boeing felt, it could beat Lockheed and McDonnell-Douglas once again.

THERE WAS, however, a wrinkle. Up until the mid-1960s, no European firm had had the means to develop a wide-bodied aircraft alone. In 1967, though, Germany, France, and Great Britain created a consortium called Airbus Industrie to build and market such a plane. The firm's structure was reflected in the construction of the first Airbus plane, the wide-bodied A-300. England made the wings and owned 20 percent of the firm. Germany made the fuselage and owned 38 percent. Spain, with the tail, owned 4 percent. France made the cockpit and owned 38 percent. A Frenchman named Bernard Lathière managed the whole affair. Like many big European enterprises, Airbus involved the active participation of government, which put up much of the financing.

But it was unique in that it included many governments, not just one. The backing of these governments—and the political stake each one had in the
firm's success—gave it a potential advantage over a
privately owned firm like Boeing.

In seven years Lathière took Airbus from nowhere
to number two in the industry. When Airbus began
production in 1974, Boeing held 75 percent of the
world market, Lockheed and McDonnell-Douglas
about 10 percent each, and small European builders
the rest. By 1980 Airbus had sold over 300 planes,
beating out the DC-10 and the L-1011 and carving
out a 35 percent share of the market. Boeing,
however, had a strong grip on the United States.
Most of the Airbus planes had been sold abroad,
often to government-owned airlines. European planes
didn't have a particularly good reputation in the
United States: American airlines complained that
European makers didn't support their aircraft with
technical assistance and spare parts. They also felt
the Europeans were too slow in delivering planes,
geared as they were to maintaining steady employment rather than to meeting peak demand.

To break into the United States, Airbus hired
George Warde, former president of American Airlines.
Warde had a unique strategy. "I decided to go to the
least likely purchaser of the airplane," he explained
later, "an American that was born in America, raised
in American society, who went to college and school
at Government-supported institutions, who was an
astronaut, and who had so much American loyalty
that if he bought a European product everybody
would think it had to be good." George Warde, in
short, went to Eastern Airlines' Frank Borman. "We
could guarantee to Borman," Lathière said, "that

compared to 727s the Airbus was better on fuel burn by between 25 and 30 percent. He knew too that the Airbus can do about the same job with two engines that the Lockheed L-1011 can do with three. So anytime he was replacing the 1011 with an Airbus he was making around $1.5 million a year in extra cash flow." Borman drove a hard bargain, insisting on a free introductory trial. But Airbus's gamble paid off: Eastern ordered 23 of the new planes, eventually upping the order to 34. Within a year Airbus had doubled its sales.

Then Boeing struck back. It sold Borman 27 of its new fuel-efficient 757s. It nosed Airbus out when it won the 767 launch order from United. And in 1979 TWA had shaken hands on an order for Airbus's new A-310 when Boeing's Commercial Division president, E. H. "Tex" Boullioun, pulled out all the stops in an effort to change TWA's mind. Boullioun wrote or telephoned TWA's board members, urging them to buy American. He promised that if his new plane didn't meet fuel-efficiency standards, Boeing would pay penalty costs. Airbus's Warde groused; Boullioun, he said, had deliberately hyped the fuel-efficiency claims for the 767 so TWA could count on getting the money. But the ploy worked. By the end of 1979 Boeing had beaten Airbus on four out of five orders and by 1981 had orders for $12 billion worth of new planes.

Still the game was not over. In 1982 the airlines, hit hard by the slumping economy, began to cancel out. American alone withdrew some $500 million in orders for the 757 and asked to delay delivery on 30 of the 767s. United wanted to cancel or delay up to 40 orders. Airbus, though it wasn't making much progress in the United States, continued to sell well abroad, eating into the markets that accounted for 60 percent of Boeing's sales. In mid 1982 Boeing had orders remaining on its books for about 300 airplanes, with an additional 200 "options," or preliminary commitments to buy. Airbus had 344 firm orders, mostly from a collection of smaller airlines, and 159 options.

Boeing's domestic competitors, meanwhile, had all but given up. Lockheed never did build the derivative of the L-1011 it had talked about and in December 1981 decided to scrap the L-1011 program entirely, phasing out production by late 1983 or early 1984. With only 244 sold, it had been a financial failure. McDonnell-Douglas was no better off. Another mishap involving the DC-10, this one in Miami, had cast a pall over the plane's sales. Instead of modifying it to meet the mid-size market, Douglas went ahead with a stretched-out version of the DC-9, called the Super-80, designed to carry at least 175 passengers. It made its debut in 1980, ahead of the 767 and the A-310, but its worldwide orders never compared with Boeing's. The company did plan a 200-seat plane to be built in collaboration with Fokker, the Dutch manufacturer, but observers felt the plane was unlikely to make it off the drawing boards. "Just as Lockheed did," said one airframe analyst, "they will have to look at their program. I think they will see they are faced with the same situation and make the same decision."

Boeing's situation, in short, was more than a little ironic. Its competitive successes in the 1970s and early 1980s had left it on top of the heap, with a virtual monopoly on the domestic commercial aircraft market. The companies it had struggled with for decades had all but yielded. Yet the slumping economy and the canceled orders meant that Boeing's workers were once again facing layoffs and its managers were once again wondering where they would find the cash necessary to finance the company's operations. And the competition, if anything, was likely to intensify. Since no buyer likes to be at the mercy of a single supplier, U.S. airlines would undoubtedly follow Eastern's lead and, when the economy recovered, would place some of their orders with Airbus. Every plane Airbus sold in the United States, moreover, would help the company sell more, as it developed sales, service, and financial relationships with the airlines. Boeing had won and won and won—only to find, like Sisyphus, that the job it now faced was just as big as ever.

UNLIKE the airframe industry, the airline industry has until recently enjoyed only a modest amount of competition. The reason was simple enough: the airlines were closely regulated by the Civil Aeronautics Board (CAB), a federal agency set up under the Roosevelt administration to rationalize the infant air-transport system. One of the board's original purposes was to forestall cutthroat competition—to prevent "competing carriers from engaging in rate wars which would be disastrous to all concerned," as the enabling legislation put it. For forty years the CAB apportioned routes among the airlines and set most fares. The result was a gray consistency from airline to airline, with little real competition among them.

By 1978, however, a movement for deregulation had begun to gather steam. Sen. Edward M. Kennedy of Massachusetts, eager to revise his image as a friend of big government and an enemy of free enterprise, was one of its leaders. Regulation, said Kennedy and his supporters, had stifled competition. The airlines could count on getting whatever fare increases they wanted from the CAB and so could waste money on gimmicks and frills that customers then had to pay for. With competition the airlines would have to fight for business. Fares would drop and service would improve.

Not everyone bought these arguments. Delta Airlines, for one, countered that deregulation would lead to the elimination of service in less profitable, smaller markets. It foresaw a wave of merger madness, with weaker airlines being swallowed up by stronger ones, and thus a decrease in consumer choice. Nevertheless, the deregulation bill had a lot of support. Conservatives couldn't easily oppose it without seeming to be a friend of government and an enemy of the marketplace. Liberals thought it was a good way both to serve consumers and to prove they too were against overregulation. Accordingly the Airline Deregulation Act of 1978 passed handily. It gave the airlines greater freedom to add or drop routes and to set fares. It also provided that the CAB itself would be phased out over the next several years.

From an airlines' point of view, the law ushered in a brand-new competitive world. A line was now free to look for new routes and to cut fares. But it would also, as Eastern discovered, have to fend off competition from aggressive new airlines eager to take on the big guys. One such was New York Air.

NEW YORK AIR'S ROOTS, ironically, weren't in New York at all but in Texas. In 1972 two 30-year-old Harvard Business School graduates named Frank

Lorenzo and Robert Carney had taken over a tiny airline called Trans-Texas Airways. Trans-Texas was something of a joke. It was sometimes called "Tinkertoy" or "Treetop" Airways by its critics because it flew obsolete planes with few customers in them to little Texas towns. It was losing $6 million a year, had $20 million in debts, and seemed destined for bankruptcy.

Lorenzo and Carney refinanced the company and almost immediately showed a profit. Within six years they had it competing fiercely with the local establishment: Braniff International, Continental, and Southwest. Soon the rickety old planes were gone and so was the old name. Texas International Airlines, with 26 DC-9s, became a small but tough and sophisticated airline with a bright future.

TIA also began aggressive efforts to take over other airlines. First it tried to buy National, then TWA, both with no luck. Finally it succeeded in acquiring Continental. The acquisition expanded its routes enormously. But the most important outcome of its takeover efforts was an immense pile of cash. It had bought up, for example, a large bloc of National stock in its first takeover attempt. Then Pan Am made an offer for National, causing the stock to shoot up in value. When Pan Am's offer was successful, Lorenzo and Carney didn't have National—but they did have a lot of money. Before long the total was $100 million, which they used to set up a holding company called Texas Air Corporation. Among Texas Air's first moves was to put $25 million into a brand-new airline with a simple objective. New York Air, as the new line was called, would challenge Eastern's legendary Air Shuttle.

Created in 1961, the Air Shuttle offered hourly

service in the heavily traveled corridors between Boston, New York, and Washington. The key to the Shuttle was not just frequency of service but guaranteed seating and ticketing on the plane. That meant a passenger could go to the airport without a reservation or a ticket, get on the plane, and pay the fare while the plane was in the air. If a plane was full, Eastern simply rolled up another. Though Eastern founder Eddie Rickenbacker had derided the Shuttle idea when it was first proposed—calling it "nothing but a damn bus service"—it rapidly became an institution. It also became an essential part of Eastern's revenue picture, providing $100 million in operating income in 1980 alone. It was not a part of its business that Eastern could afford to take lightly.

New York Air's plan was to operate a shuttlelike service of its own in the same corridors. The fares, however, would be much lower: $39 on the Boston to New York route as against $56 for the Shuttle, and $49 on the New York to Washington route as against $59 for the Shuttle. The key to this strategy was lower costs. New York Air owned only 6 of its 13 old DC-9s, leasing the rest, so it didn't have the capital costs Eastern had. More important, it had no union labor. Eastern pilots earned as much as $75,000 a year; New York Air's, with no union status and less seniority, would earn about $30,000. Flight attendants and ticketing staff would make less as well. And the absence of union work rules would allow the airline to get more productivity from its employees. New York Air's pilots, for example, would be expected to fly 70 hours a month instead of the 52 hours Eastern's pilots flew.

In December 1980 New York Air launched its

service. A special fare of $29 one-way to both Boston and Washington had generated a lot of publicity; so had the young airline's substantial ad campaign. Eastern fought back. It lowered its fare on weekends and intensified its own advertising. It could not, however, go too far. "Load factor," as airline people call it, is the average number of seats filled on each flight. The lower the price, the higher the load factor required for profitability. Eastern knew that it couldn't make up in load factor what it was giving up in price, so there was a limit as to how far it could cut fares.

At first things looked good for New York Air. In March 1981—three months after it began flying—the airline drew 28 percent of the total New York–Boston–Washington market. Eastern was down only 8 percent from the previous year—the rest of New York Air's gain had evidently come from trains, cars, and other airlines—but a spokesman said the Shuttle's profits were "marginal." Then, in August, the air traffic controllers went out on strike. The secretary of transportation announced a 25 percent cut in flights from congested airports. That helped Eastern's cause considerably. It could compensate for losing some of its flights by using big A-300 airbuses between Boston and New York, though not between New York and Washington, because wide-bodied planes are banned from Washington's National Airport. So it could carry just as many passengers with fewer flights on that route. New York Air, with only DC-9s to draw on, had to cancel its Boston–to–New York service.

In 1982 the fare-cutting ended. New York Air raised its fares early in the year from $49 to $55 on the New York–to–Washington run. Eastern went up to $60 on that route and to $55 on Boston to New York. The strike, the slumping economy, and Eastern's resistance all had hit New York Air hard, throwing it into the red for the last two quarters of 1981 and forcing it both to raise fares and to borrow money. Shut out of the New York–to–Boston route, the line began serving cities that it had intended to get to later—Buffalo, Cincinnati, Baltimore. "We're not retreating," said New York Air's president, Neal Meehan, "just fighting in a different direction." Eastern, meanwhile, had regained its near-monopoly on New York–to–Boston shuttle-style flights. But the recession and competitive pressures on its other routes meant that it too was facing hard times.

NEW YORK AIR was just one example of changing times in the airline industry. "It's almost as if Texas Air Corporation is setting up a franchise operation," said industry analyst Michael Derchin of Oppenheimer & Company. "It's an interesting concept, setting up pockets of new service in various parts of the country and undercutting the incumbent carrier with low fares." Howard Putnam, the president of Texas Air's bitter rival, Southwest Airlines, explained the implication. "You have to specialize and find a niche these days. They don't give out medals anymore just for flying all over the place and being big."

Finding the niche, however, can be hard, and the story of New York Air and Eastern was played out, in different settings, throughout the industry. Chicago-based Midway Airlines, for example, hit the headlines in 1979, offering fares up to 50 percent lower than those of the big airlines with which it was competing. At first, according to a *New York Times* report, the big carriers ignored Midway, claiming it didn't have enough capacity to threaten them. Then at one point Midway "offered $60 in cash to passengers with standard, full-cost tickets on other airlines if they used those tickets to fly with Midway." This ploy upped Midway's market share to between 35 and 40 percent, and the big lines struck back. First they matched Midway's low fares. Then they canceled the "interline" agreement under which they had honored tickets and handled baggage for Midway's passengers (and those of other small lines) at no charge. Under these competitive pressures, Midway's load factor dropped from a high near 65 percent in mid-1981 to a low around 45 percent in early 1982. Its president, however, told the *Times* that the line was better situated than the major carriers to ride out a price war. Like New York Air, it utilized nonunion labor, secondhand planes, and a variety of other cost-cutting strategies.

Elsewhere, lines like People Express, Muse Air, Columbia, and Air Chicago jumped into major markets using tactics much like New York Air's and Midway's, with varying degrees of success. The big carriers, moreover, began to take on each other in a kind of cutthroat competition that was reminiscent of the railroads' early days. Pan Am, which suffered losses of $217 million in 1980, began offering cuts up to 67 percent on all domestic economy-class tickets. The price of a ticket from New York to Los Angeles, for example, went from $498 to $219. TWA cut the price of a New York–Miami fare from $99 to $69, and it joined United and Capital in cutting one-way, night-flight fares between New York and San Francisco to $99. That rate was considerably below even a $133 Greyhound bus ticket.

In general those who favored deregulation have been elated by such results. The CAB's Office of Economic Analysis reported, two years after the law passed, that "deregulation had brought about fundamental changes in the industry, which will continue to bring better, lower-cost air travel to the vast majority of air travelers." Yale University economist Paul W. MacAvoy, a specialist in regulated industries, agreed. "Where passenger demand has grown most, principally in travel within and to the South and West," he wrote in The New York Times, "virtually all cities have new service, fare discounts, and a greater choice of flights. There are more than a dozen new airlines flying jets and more than 700 routes in the country have old or new airlines providing service for the first time. The shorter, low-density routes have gotten less service from the scheduled carriers, but more from commuter carriers with flights up more than 50 percent [in one year]."

There was, however, some question as to whether the competition could continue. Like New York Air, most of the small airlines were hard hit by the controllers' strike and the resulting reduction in flights. Observers doubted too how long the small lines' advantages could last. Peter Nulty wrote in Fortune in early 1981: "As staff seniority accumulates, labor costs on new airlines will increase, wiping out some of their original advantage. Southwest, only ten years old, pays salaries comparable to the industry average, though it still flies with fewer pilots who spend more time in the air. The Air Line Pilots Association claims that it is not upset by the recent upsurge of non-union shops; they will be organized over time." Certainly the pilots had lost no time in taking on New York Air. Charging that it was nothing but a runaway shop—a ruse for Texas International to escape its labor agreements—the ALPA had picketed and sued New York Air in federal court. "They're just repainting Texas International planes and sending them to New York," said an ALPA spokesman. "What's to prevent them from repainting them again and sending them back to Texas as a wholly owned subsidiary of New York Air?"

There were other worries, too, both for the airlines and for the consumers. Was it safe for the smaller lines to be flying their pilots 72 hours a month? Would the financial pressures induce the airlines to cut corners on maintenance and aircraft safety inspections? And while economy fares were slashed, fares often went up for daytime customers or those on less heavily traveled routes. The airlines, in alienating their regular business, might be cutting off their noses to spite their faces.

The chief concern for the airlines, however, was simply that they were losing money hand over fist. In the first year of deregulation the scheduled airlines' profits dropped 80 percent. In 1980 all the airlines together lost a net of $225 million, and in 1981 the eight losers among the top ten airlines racked up losses totaling $824 million. Pan Am won the prize with a $360 million deficit, but Continental, American, and United lost anywhere from $40 to $140 million each. Braniff's fate was still worse. "The first fatality of deregulation was Braniff International, which until 1979 had been among the most prosperous of the big airlines," writes John Newhouse in The Sporty Game, an account of the industry published in 1982. "Braniff played under the new rules more lustily than any other big airline, expanding its operations to an astonishing degree, and in so doing destroyed itself." As early as 1981 Neal Effmen, a TWA vice-president, had said, "I'm not sure who can win this war. We may all end up as losers." His words were beginning to sound prescient.

Faced with such losses, the airlines were quietly relieved by the 25 percent cut-in-flights order that followed the traffic controllers' strike. In effect the order was regulation through fiat: it essentially froze the number of flights that many airlines could offer, and it ensured that each flight would be more nearly filled up. The business commentator Frederick Thayer noted in a December 1981 article that "the air traffic controllers have rescued the airlines from the ravages of deregulation"—though for Braniff, at least, the worst was still to come. In any event, a movement for re-regulation seemed to be gaining ground, particularly among the worst-off airlines. "For years fares were too high," said World Airways' president, Edward Daly, in 1982. "Now they are too low, and I will not remain silent." Daly, who had been an early supporter of deregulation, was now calling on the CAB to "assume leadership in ending the disastrous and completely irrational fare wars."

"THE SAD TRUTH," said the *New York Times* editorialist Peter Passell in commenting on Daly's pronouncement, "is that competition doesn't always get you exactly where you want to go." It was better, Passell thought, than government regulation, but it had its costs. Among them was the possibility that a lot of airlines—particularly younger, more aggressive ones without "deep enough pockets"—would be driven out of business by all the fare cutting.

Low fares might benefit the consumer in the short run, but—just as opponents of deregulation had once prophesied—in the long run might actually reduce the consumer's choice. Unbridled competition might continue until the biggest and strongest airlines had cut the throats of all the smaller ones and had the market to themselves. That, of course, is essentially what happened in the airframe industry. What started as a competition with shifting leaders in the commercial aircraft market ended, in 1980, with Boeing controlling most of the market and its two domestic competitors all but out of the game. Only the rise of international competition kept Boeing from occupying the marketplace essentially all by itself.

In the real world, therefore, "cutthroat" competition can be hard to distinguish from market-share competition. What begins as one form may wind up as the other, depending on the changing conditions of the marketplace and depending on the relative success of the competitors as they pursue their diverse strategies. The only safe conclusion is that, just as nature abhors a vacuum, a market economy abhors an absence of competition. Airbus grew large precisely because Boeing's other competitors had left the field wide open. And if Airbus didn't exist, it would probably soon be invented. No airline would want to be dependent on Boeing as its sole supplier, and any company, government, or consortium with sufficient access to capital would find itself tempted by the prospect of tapping the multi-billion-dollar airframe industry. Nowhere can this pressure toward competition be seen more clearly than in the airline business. What for years had been a sleepy, mostly prosperous industry was suddenly transformed by deregulation into a scrambling entrepreneurial battlefield with a host of new entrants.

As both examples show, competition cuts two ways. A highly competitive industry is one where profits and jobs are continually in jeopardy—where companies frequently focus their efforts only on products or services that promise immediate profits or, on the contrary, where they are forced by the competition into unprofitable operations, and where long-term planning can often take a back seat to whatever is necessary for the company to stay alive. An industry in which competition is muted is often the reverse. Firms that enjoy relatively safe market positions have the time and money necessary for long-term investments, research and development, generous employment policies, and other expensive luxuries. From the consumer's perspective, though, competition is the only thing that is sure to keep an enterprise on its toes. It is easy, in a noncompetitive industry, for firms to charge more than competitive prices or to grow lax in their service. When the competition is stiff, both price and quality are top priority. The consumer, if not the worker or the shareholder, usually benefits.

It is competition, finally, that gives the market its dynamism. No one can say that Boeing will not, in the next ten years, be displaced by Airbus—or that both won't be challenged by some new competitor. Similarly, no one can foresee the future of the airlines. New York Air may succeed in upending Eastern or some other giant on some of its routes, or it may be forced to retreat to Texas to lick its wounds. Eastern itself will have to hope it can pull itself out of its doldrums and stave off the competition at the same time. Like any enterprise, big or small, it can't take the future for granted.

Moreover, if Eastern, Boeing, or any other big company stays down and vulnerable long enough, its competitors will not necessarily help it back on its feet, like basketball players aiding an injured opponent. They may, like boxers, try instead to keep it down for the count.

"WORKING WITH PEOPLE is difficult," Peter Drucker once said, "but not impossible." Certainly many companies have foundered on the rocks of poor organization. Management squabbles, poor labor relations, high turnover rates—all are symptoms of a company where people are working at cross-purposes instead of together. The effect of such disarray can be just as devastating for a company as failure to develop new products or failure to meet the competition.

Firms that run smoothly, by contrast, are frequently noted for their business success. IBM's reputation as a "great company to work for," as one dispassionate report had it, is not the only reason for its dominance in electronics. But neither has it hurt. Particularly in an industry where people jump ship a lot anyway to start their own firms, high morale and job satisfaction pay off.

In many Americans' eyes, the success of the Japanese can be traced to their notion of the company as a family, in which workers are treated as human beings and in turn are devoted to their employer. The pervasiveness of the Japanese model can be overstated: even in Japan it characterizes only the larger firms. But again there is little doubt that it has contributed to these very firms' phenomenal success in international markets. Japanese productivity and workmanship are known throughout the world.

Can the Japanese model be exported? The experience of a Japanese-owned company in San Diego answers this question with a resounding maybe. As the next chapter shows, Americans have traditions and expectations of their own when it comes to running an organization, and grafting on the style of a different culture isn't always easy.

Yet, as Drucker might have put it, it isn't impossible either.

8. Working

THE YOUNG JAPANESE sales manager raised a cup of sake in a toast to his fellow employees in the production department. "From sales," he began grandly, "I would like to say we trust you, we have confidence in you." He paused for effect, then continued. "I don't know if we like you or not." The mixed crowd of Japanese and Americans around him laughed tentatively as he finished the salute. "We feel that we're all part of the same family, you are ours and we are yours. Please let's work together in 1981."

A moment of awkward silence followed the toast. Then the audience applauded politely.

This was the start of a Japanese *compa*, literally "companion meeting," a gathering through which Japanese colleagues in an enterprise try to resolve conflict. The participants were employees of Kyocera, a firm located in San Diego but owned by a Japanese company. Shortly before, Kyocera had received a big new order from Western Electric for the tiny ceramic chip carriers that were its chief product. But trouble had developed in fulfilling the order. Bob Osmun, the sales executive in charge of the Western Electric account, was afraid that the people running the so-called 560 Advanced Package Division didn't realize how large the order would eventually be. Production, long accustomed to short runs, might not be up to fulfilling Western Electric's sizable order on schedule. At the *compa*, sales manager Jim Uyeda was expressing his hope that the two divisions could work together more fruitfully from then on.

As the evening wore on, reserve gave way to friendliness and eventually to raucousness. The *compa* that night ended with several of the Japanese swaying happily to the rhythm of their company song, which they roared out in their native tongue. "The morning glory of the dawning sky is approaching," the song runs, "much like an orchestra playing a symphony . . . with overflowing youth and energy we bear the banner of our principle to carry out our mission all over the five continents of the world." The Americans, grinning, looked on.

MOST BUSINESSES are more than a one-person operation. The entrepreneur or manager running the business thus has to make sure that everyone in the organization is working together as effectively as possible. Though simply stated, the task is complex. It subsumes what usually goes under the headings of labor relations, personnel management, and so on. But it is broader than these labels indicate. As the Kyocera example suggests, the problem of maintaining an effective organization can crop up at any level of a company in a dozen different settings.

American firms have inherited two distinct traditions of running an organization. In recent years they have begun to look longingly at the Japanese model as a third choice. Styles of management, however, can't be imported as easily as cameras. As the history of the American approaches to management reveals, Westerners are not always prepared to confront the task of reshaping the workplace. And as Kyocera's experience shows, the Japanese may be more successful at running their own plants than they are at exporting their methods.

Like many of the issues explored in this book, the problem of managing a sizable business enterprise is relatively new in history. For much of the nineteenth century most firms in America employed no more than ten or twenty people. Only a small fraction of the working population were wage laborers; the rest were farmers, craftsmen, small businessmen, merchants, and professionals. Even the first large enterprises didn't always employ workers in the same way they are employed today. Andrew Carnegie's Homestead Steel Works, for example, was run until 1892 largely by an association of skilled craftsmen known as the Amalgamated Association of Iron, Steel, and Tin Workers. "The skilled workers who dominated the union worked much like independent contractors," as one writer puts it. "They produced steel with company equipment but largely according to (association) rules, and they hired and paid their own unskilled help."

But the steel mill illustrated a problem. Without direct control over the deployment of men and machines, company managers couldn't easily cut costs

when business conditions demanded it. Carnegie's
managers wanted to introduce new machines and
reduce the labor force; the craftsmen and their employees resisted. In 1892 Carnegie finally abolished
the system entirely. The association went on strike
and a battle ensued. But Pennsylvania's governor,
Robert E. Pattison, sent 7,000 troops to Homestead
to oust the strikers, and shortly the mill was re-
opened with new workers. The issue of "whether
the Carnegie Company or the Amalgamated Association shall have absolute control of our plant and
business at Homestead," as Carnegie manager Henry
Clay Frick had phrased it, was resolved in favor of
management.

The attempt to control the labor force directly and
thereby to keep costs in line found its greatest ex-
pression in the work of Frederick Winslow Taylor.
Taylor was the son of a well-known Philadelphia
lawyer and went to school at Exeter and Harvard.
When a nervous breakdown cut short his plans for a
law career, he took a job at the Midvale Steel Works
in northern Philadelphia as a journeyman machinist.
Six years later he had become chief engineer. Along
the way he confronted a problem that had plagued
not only Midvale's managers but the managers of
many other mills and factories in the United States.

In the days before the assembly line, workers themselves necessarily controlled much of the work
process. "Foremen determined how jobs were to be
done," writes the historian Elisha P. Douglass, "and
the workers determined in practice if not in theory
the time necessary to accomplish them." If wages
were paid by the day, the workers worked a little
slower. So companies often paid workers by the
piece, on the assumption that since faster and more

efficient workers would make more money, output would go up. But piece rates brought their own problems. "Employers tended to reduce the piecework rate when it became apparent that a given job could be accomplished in a shorter time," explains Douglass; "workmen, in an attempt to maintain the rate, slowed their pace accordingly."

Taylor was "convinced that output per worker would never rise until management took the responsibility for establishing shop procedures and planning output down to the smallest detail." So he carried out a series of studies designed to measure exactly how long each job should take. That set a standard whereby management could establish piecework rates and workers could meet them without fear that they would then be lowered. Taylor also established a differential rate system that rewarded workers who produced more with a higher rate per piece.

In 1895 he gave a paper detailing the Midvale system and laying out the principles of what would soon be known as scientific management. It wasn't long before he was America's most prominent industrial relations expert. By the turn of the century scientific management itself had become almost a cult. It was viewed, reports Douglass, "as a method of reorganizing production methods which had profound implications for widespread transformation of basic social and economic relationships."

Taylor's basic goal was more modest. It was simply to extract from each employee a "fair day's work"—"all the work," as he defined it, "a worker can do without injury to his health, at a pace that can be sustained throughout a working lifetime." To this end he developed three fundamental principles.

First, the work process was to be subdivided. Managers would be the only ones who understood how a given operation worked and would assign employees discrete functions "independent of craft, tradition, and the worker's knowledge."

Second—a related principle, and one that Taylor considered "the key to scientific management"—was the separation of the conceptualization of work from its execution. "All possible brain work," he wrote, "should be removed from the shop and centered in the planning or laying-out department." This separation, Taylor thought, would lead to substantial savings. Its possibilities would be realized only when "almost all of the machines in the shop are run by men who are of smaller calibre and attainments and who are therefore cheaper than those required under the old system."

Third, Taylor assumed that managers, freed from the need to supervise workers directly, would exercise rational control over all aspects of the production process. Scientific management thus did much to create and legitimate the role of the professional manager. So too did the business school, the first of which (the University of Pennsylvania's Wharton School) appeared in 1881. With the rationalization of production came the notion that a worker's job was to work and a manager's job was to manage.

The technological apogee of scientific management arrived with the assembly line, introduced by Ransom E. Olds (creator of the Oldsmobile) and first installed on a large scale by Henry Ford. When the Ford Motor Company started production near the turn of the century, most of its workers were skilled craftsmen who built and finished whole sections of a car. The vehicle was assembled in one place, with workers bringing in parts and assemblies as needed. Borrowing from Olds, Ford decided to reverse the process—"taking the work to the men instead of the men to the work," as he described it—and built his new Highland Park plant around the concept of production lines. In 1913 two Ford technicians at the Highland Park factory introduced the idea of a moving conveyor. Using a windlass, they experimented with dragging the automobile's chassis across the floor. That cut assembly time for a car from 12.5 hours to just under 6. Then, replacing the windlass with a mechanized overhead conveyor belt, they got it down to 1.5 hours.

Taylor evidently was not the cold, calculating manipulator of labor he is sometimes made out to be. His writings indicate that he sympathized with the era's critics of child labor and unhealthy working conditions. In making the factory more efficient, he aimed not only at increasing profits but at bettering the worker's life. "Under scientific management," he wrote, "arbitrary power, arbitrary dictation ceases ... (and) the man at the head of the business ... is governed by rules and laws which have been developed through hundreds of experiments." At Ford the results were mixed. Production increased dramatically, allowing the company to sell its cars cheaply and thereby to dominate the young industry. And Ford more than doubled the minimum wage, paying his workers $5 a day and offering the famous explanation that he could sell more cars if his employees could afford to buy them. The employees, however, seem to have been less than enthusiastic about the new production process. By 1913 the company was experiencing a turnover rate of 380 percent. Employees who remained grumbled, in spite of the high wages, and some began talking up the idea of a union.

Unions themselves were considerably longer in coming to the American scene than is commonly realized. Labor history is ordinarily traced back to the founding of the Knights of Labor in 1869. But for many years unions in most industries were weak, short-lived, or simply nonexistent. "Trade unions that sought to reduce the hours of labor or to improve wage rates," writes the historian Sidney Fine of nineteenth-century America, "were reminded that matters of this sort were determined by inexorable laws of supply and demand that unions, as well as employers, were powerless to set aside." Other employers greeted unions with rather more violent reminders. The history of the labor movement is rife with stories of battles fought between would-be unionists and company guards, police, or even troops.

What changed the situation for unions was, of course, the National Labor Relations Act, or the Wagner Act as it is usually called, passed in 1935. Already the government had given some protection to union organizers, notably through the Norris-LaGuardia Act and Section 7a of the National Industrial Recovery Act. But the Wagner Act not only established workers' right to organize a union, it created a process through which union certification elections could be held, overseen, and policed by a government agency known as the National Labor Relations Board. As a result union membership skyrocketed, from 3.4 million in 1930 to 8.7 million ten years later and to 14.3 million in 1950. By the end of the 1940s, unions were solidly entrenched in most of the industries where they can be found today. All told, unions represent about a fifth of the total labor force. But the percentage is substantially higher in many parts of the economy, including the so-called basic industries like automobiles and steel.

Unlike many of their counterparts in Europe, American unions have in modern times been resolutely oriented toward bread-and-butter issues. Though the AFL-CIO and many individual unions support candidates for public office, there is no labor party of the sort that exists in most European countries. Nor are unions typically concerned with on-the-job matters other than wages, hours, and working conditions. In effect unions are a sort of complement to scientific management, and the two together define the dominant theme in American industrial relations. Production is highly organized, with tasks endlessly subdivided. Employees are often well paid, but they are expected to do their jobs and not to think. By common consent, and often by union contract, control over the work process resides exclusively in the hands of management. Management in turns runs the organization in some respects as the officers run an army unit, expecting to be obeyed.

THOUGH MOST BUSINESSES have been run according to the conventional managerial model, there is another tradition that weaves its way through the history of American labor relations. Cropping up now and again in diverse forms, it is variously called the "human relations" school, "Theory Y," or in some instances "participative" management. It has turned on the fundamental idea that workers are more than machines: that they are people whose functions are more than mechanical and whose needs are more than economic.

The first sociological experiment that suggested Taylorism might be missing something was conducted in the 1920s at the Hawthorne Works of the Western Electric Company in Chicago. The subjects of the experiment were employees of a department known as the Relay Assembly Test Room. Their job consisted of arranging about thirty-five small parts and screwing them together to make remote-control switches called relays. Each relay took about a minute to assemble.

The researchers initially set out to discover whether improving working conditions would boost the worker's productivity—in particular, whether an improvement in lighting would lead to increased output. They found that output did indeed increase in the course of the experiment, but that the increase had nothing to do with the lighting. When lighting was improved, output went up. When it was decreased, output went up again.

Curiosity piqued, the researchers joined up with a group from the Harvard Business School to test a string of other variables. They divided the experiment into periods of anywhere from two to thirty-one weeks apiece and measured output as the new variables were introduced. The variables included minor measures such as providing snacks or changing the length and frequency of rest periods. They also included more substantial ones, such as altering the length of working days or the working week. Yet regardless of which variables were changed or when, output almost always continued to rise. After more than a year all the changes were canceled, and workers returned to their original working conditions. Again output was higher than at any time during the experiment.

The puzzled researchers looked for other factors that might have influenced the outcome: an increase in workers' skill, less fatigue, and so on. None of these seemed to account for the change. The only one that did was a variable the researchers hadn't counted on. Output was going up, it seemed, simply because the employees were more and more satisfied with their work. As sociologist Paul Blumberg analyzed the results in his book *Industrial Democracy*, the Relay Test Room Assembly workers got three critical opportunities not ordinarily afforded their fellow workers. They got a break from customary discipline. They were allowed the latitude to do their jobs any way they choose. And they were involved with the researchers in designing the experiments. All three, Blumberg speculates, contributed to a rise in job satisfaction and thus to productivity. An earlier observer, Stuart Chase, came to the same conclusion. The relay workers "found stability, a place where they belonged, and work whose purpose they could clearly see. And so they worked faster and better than they ever had in their lives."

"The Hawthorne studies," says one business textbook, "revolutionized management's approach to direction (or motivation) of employees." That may be an overstatement, but there is little doubt that the experiments signaled a new theme in industrial relations. Before, as the business historian Thomas C. Cochran puts it, managerial authority was thought to be based on the operation of natural law: "success was a proof of virtue, and failure to rise from the ranks of labor showed a lack of either intelligence or proper moral qualities. The inevitable trend of the new psychology was to make management partially responsible for the success or failure of workers, to replace the inexorable authority of natural law with the uncertainties of social relations." As part of this trend, companies began to employ counselors for workers with problems, to establish company magazines and pension plans, even to hire industrial psychologists to come up with ways to improve worker morale. Such experiments, says Cochran, were limited in number, but they nevertheless marked "the beginning of the breakdown in labor relations of the simple philosophy of the nineteenth century."

After World War II a few big companies began to experiment with redesigning work itself, again with the aim of increasing output through job satisfaction and higher morale on the part of workers. These "job-enlargement" programs gave semiskilled workers the chance to learn new skills and perform more complex tasks. Most were apparently successful. One home-laundry equipment manufacturing plant, for example, reorganized part of its production to allow workers to assemble entire water pumps or control panels at a bench instead of working on the assembly line. "More than two-thirds preferred the enlarged job," Blumberg reports. "What the workers liked about the new system was that: they now had a variety of jobs to perform; they could complete an entire operation; they could take responsibility and be given credit for the quality of their work; they weren't tied to a work station." Yet it turned out that the experiments faced at least one major obstacle and sometimes two. As job enlargement increased production, it often led to a reduction in the work force. Employees, fearful for their jobs, came to mistrust management's motives. At the same time, lower-level and middle managers frequently felt threatened by reforms that appeared to undermine their authority, perhaps even to jeopardize *their* jobs. The introduction of a job-enlargement scheme was thus a potential source of conflict as well as satisfaction. Therefore, such experiments remained the exception rather than the rule.

The ideas, however, did not die out. In 1960 a psychologist named Douglas McGregor published an influential book called *The Human Side of Enterprise*. McGregor christened the old style of labor relations—based on mindless work, close supervision, and coercion—"Theory X." In its place he proposed what he called Theory Y. Theory Y assumed that workers did not dislike work; that workers would seek out responsibility, given the chance; and that tight control and punishment systems were usually counterproductive. Though developed in the 1950s, McGregor's ideas fit easily with the wave of social reform that swept over the nation in the 1960s. They also appealed to managers wondering how best to control the younger, less obedient workers who were beginning to appear in the plants.

Many of the last two decades' experiments in industrial relations drew on McGregor's ideas. Variously called job enrichment, workers' participation plans, or simply "quality of working life" experiments, they tried to involve workers in doing more, thinking more, and taking more responsibility. At a Harman International Industries automobile-mirror plant in southwestern Tennessee, for example, management and the United Auto Workers jointly designed a system to reorganize production. The key to the plan was a series of discussion groups, called core groups, aimed at eliciting workers' ideas as to how work could be improved. In one department, according to one report, groups of workers "decided to see if they could work in teams, to determine among themselves such things as who would do what job, to keep their own records, and to cover for each other when one team member was absent." The result was an increase in production so dramatic that some department workers would leave the plant each day several hours earlier than before. Thanks to the union's involvement, there was no danger that production quotas would simply be upped to reflect the new output levels.

Similar experiments took place elsewhere: in a deep coal mine in central Pennsylvania, in a New York hospital, in a pet-food plant in Topeka. Most found that both productivity and worker satisfaction went up whenever the workplace was reshaped to allow for greater freedom. Most ran into some of the same obstacles that had plagued their earlier counterparts. Supervisors and some workers felt threatened; one critical worker at the mirror plant, for instance, charged that "there was too much daydreaming about things down the road" and argued that the program hadn't dealt with the plant's worst physical problems. Old-line managers feared raising their workers' expectations too far. And with a few exceptions like the United Auto Workers, unions remained hostile or uncooperative, mistrusting management's motives. Despite its successes, the Theory Y approach made only a few inroads.

As the 1970s progressed, though, it slowly dawned on American business that things were not what they once had been in the U.S. economy. Productivity was rising only slowly. Absenteeism and turnover remained high. Growth rates were lower than those in many other industrial nations. The powerful West German economy was coming to dominate much of Europe. And Japan, the fastest-growing industrial economy in the world, was threatening to dominate not only Asia but America itself. The statistics in autos alone suggested the story. In 1965 the United States imported only 6 percent of the automobiles sold. Fifteen years later the figure had roughly quadrupled, to the point where about a quarter of all new cars were foreign made. In steel, electronics, and half a dozen other areas the trend was similar. America was being outstripped by its former enemy.

As JAPAN GREW in economic prominence, so too did Americans' interest in why Japan was so successful. Books like Ezra Vogel's *Japan as Number One* and William Ouchi's *Theory Z: How American Business Can Meet the Japanese Challenge* began to turn up on business school assignment lists and in executive suites. Americans wondered what they could learn from the Japanese.

One source of the Japanese economy's phenomenal growth were laws and policies specifically designed to promote growth. The original supply-siders, the Japanese tax both corporate and personal incomes less than the United States does, and they dispense entirely with capital gains taxes on securities. The famed Ministry of Trade and Industry (MITI) gives generous allotments of research-and-development money to promising industries and helps coordinate research efforts among competing companies. In the high-tech industry, for example, MITI at one point brought together five firms to coordinate the development of state-of-the-art circuitry for computers. It also controls industrial standards and product licensing in such a way as to delineate markets.

Structurally and culturally, most Japanese companies are oriented toward growth more than American firms. Banks, for example, may own up to 5 percent of the stock of major corporations—a practice forbidden in this country—and interlocking directorates among banks and businesses are encouraged. As a result, Japanese firms can count on long-term, beneficial credit arrangements and thus depend heavily on borrowed capital. According to a Chase Manhattan study, this difference means that Japanese firms can prosper with only three-fifths of the return on investment that a typical American company requires. And according to a report in The New York Times, profit itself is not so highly valued in Japan as in the United States. Rather, a company is likely to evaluate its performance by reference to its share of the market. Pricing policies and long-term plans designed to facilitate growth are thus encouraged, even at the expense of short-term profitability.

The most significant difference between Japanese companies and American ones, however, seems to turn on industrial relations, as reflected in the attitudes and performance of workers. Large firms in Japan (though not smaller ones) hire many of their workers for life. Employees are paid relatively low wages but are given bonuses at the end of the year reflecting the company's profits; these bonuses may amount to a substantial fraction of the worker's compensation. The workers thus have an interest not only in the firm's profitability but, secure in the knowledge that their jobs aren't in jeopardy, in adapting to new production techniques. These economic differences can be traced to differences in culture. The corporation involves itself with every aspect of a Japanese worker's life; the worker in turn is expected to feel a familial loyalty to the company. Exercises, songs, and other rituals reinforce these feelings of mutual identification.

Signs of the difference in attitude and culture pervade Japanese factories—and are more noticeable, observers say, than any futuristic technological innovations such as robots. An American plant, typically, is noisy, dirty, a little unruly. Parts may be piled up awaiting assembly. Foremen and plant managers may be racing from crisis to crisis, unscrambling bottlenecks or hurriedly ordering supplies. The Japanese plant presents the opposite picture. "The factories I visited," writes Robert H. Hayes, a Harvard Business School professor, "were unexpectedly quiet and orderly, regardless of the type of industry, the age of a company, its location, or whether it was a U.S. subsidiary." They were also, he says, exceptionally clean. "Sources of litter and grime were carefully controlled: boxes placed to catch metal shavings, plastic tubes and pipes positioned to catch and direct oil away from the workplace, spare parts and raw materials carefully stored in specified areas. The rest areas were centrally located, tastefully decorated (often with plants and flowers), and immaculate."

Other differences appeared to Hayes as well. One was the Japanese system of avoiding large inventories of parts and materials. "Work was meted out to the plant in careful doses instead of being, as one U.S. manager put it, 'dumped on the floor so the foreman can figure out what to do with it.'" There was rarely an atmosphere of crisis, such as often characterizes American plants at the end of a week or the end of a month. And everything seemed designed to ensure quality in the final product—"zero defects," as the Japanese put it. " 'Pursuing the last grain of rice in the corner of the lunchbox' is a Japanese saying that describes, somewhat disparagingly, a person's tendency to be overscrupulous," Hayes writes. "But it conveys volumes about the Japanese character. As managers and as workers, the Japanese are smart and industrious—and never satisfied. They regard *all* problems as important."

KYOTO CERAMICS, Kyocera's parent company, is in some ways unique but in many other ways typical of the large Japanese firm. Its founder, Kazuo Inamori, has always been unusual. His teenage dream was to be a Kamikaze pilot. And where the typical Japanese manager joins a company and stays on for life, Inamori left his first job in his early twenties after a disagreement with his boss. Soon thereafter he started Kyoto, with a stake variously reported at $5,000 to $10,000. Today he is one of the richest men in Japan. By 1980 he owned affiliates on three continents. From 1975 through 1981 his company's annual sales rose almost sevenfold to $681 million. Profits soared more than fourfold, up to $68 million.

Kyoto specializes in high-grade industrial ceramics made from the refined chemicals found in clay. Ceramics are hard, strong, heat resistant, and electrically nonconducting. They can be adapted for a wide variety of products ranging from semiconductor housings to artificial bones. Kyoto, not wanting to overspecialize, has experimented with uses for ceramics in automobile engines, solar cells, and synthetic gems. But the company's largest item by far is ceramic castings for semiconductors, representing nearly half their total sales in 1981.

In its approach to workers, Kyoto is typical of the large Japanese firm. Women make up 40 percent of the company's labor force, but they ordinarily work only with other women. Just out of high school, most of them will work in the factories and live in dormitories until they leave the company to marry. Male employees are hired for a lifetime of employment. The policy requires both company and workers to be flexible: in times of plenty the lean work force is likely to be asked to work overtime, while in hard times they may be asked to move off the assembly line and assume maintenance jobs. At the morning roll call the names of absentees are announced to shame those who haven't shown up for work. Workers wear the same blue uniform and do exercises every day. All are not only more disciplined than Americans, they are also better informed about the company's performance. At the managerial level the company hires college graduates from the middle of the class rather than the top. It doesn't want standouts; it wants team players grateful for an opportunity.

If Inamori began as a radical, he is a diehard conservative today. Exercising tight control over his far-flung multinational empire, he is seen as father, teacher, philosopher-king, almost a kind of modern-day shogun. His managers attribute his success to his ability to inspire employees. Inamori himself adds to this view a characteristically Japanese observation: "I think there is one thing that American businessmen can learn by studying Japanese businessmen. The Japanese manage by valuing the heart of people."

* * *

IN JAPAN, the system works well. When East meets West, however, the outcome is more ambiguous. Kyocera arrived in the United States in 1971, bringing some of its managers along with it from Japan. Soon it had about 2,000 employees and was recognized as the most successful of the four major high-tech firms in San Diego. After several years, though, its performance lagged. A precipitous drop in profits in 1980 was due mostly to slump in the semiconductor industry in the United States. Still, it was during this period that Kyocera was regularly sending orders back to the mother plant in Kyoto. There the Japanese workers seemed better able to get the orders produced.

A visitor to Kyocera's plant is struck with the strange mixture of Japanese and American practices. The company did away with the strict Japanese dress code because of Americans' dislike of uniforms, but workers still must wear smocks and managers blue jackets. An American engineer fresh out of Ohio State helps the Japanese managers greet the arrival of a new $300,000 kiln with a Shinto ceremony designed to exorcise any evil spirits that may have accompanied the kiln on its journey. Workers begin work with a short meeting announcing the month's productivity figures. The announcement is accompanied by exhortations aimed at increasing output.

Like a Japanese firm, the company pursues a no-layoff policy and in fact has never laid a worker off during its more than ten years of operation in San Diego. The company makes what labor adjustments it can by not hiring replacements when its workers leave. And it is extremely careful about hiring new ones. Jobs are created only when managers have ascertained, for example, that no workers are available for transfer from other divisions. Candidates for jobs are carefully screened and once accepted are taught the Kyocera philosophy. Partly because of all this, the company's turnover rate is one of the lowest in manufacturing—and three union drives have been defeated at the plant. "I feel that a union wouldn't be too good with the family structure that we have," explained one employee.

Kyocera's performance on the big Western Electric order that occasioned the *compa* described above symbolizes both the strengths and weaknesses of the company's approach. The order was for hundreds of thousands of "chip carriers"—tiny prewired packages for computer chips, designed to connect each chip to a system while protecting it from contaminants and intense heat. Each carrier had to undergo a seven-stage production process, repetitive and potentially boring but demanding exact attention to detail. Tiny mistakes could ruin whole batches of carriers, so each had to be carefully inspected. The more rejected batches, of course, the more delays.

The first step, in good Japanese fashion, was exhortation. "We're a little bit behind on this package," a manager told the workers, "so we have to catch up. If we don't catch up, we're going to have to work some extra overtime. Okay, you've all done a very good job and I want you all to be very proud." As the order went forward, quality control became an issue. Quality-control technicians could reject any batch, even though they had passed inspection by a division manager—and too many batches were being rejected. Again, exhortation. "Our product cannot afford to have a slight mistake, because it is a great loss for our company and a great loss for us too," supervisor Minerva Bernales said. "We must love our job."

Love, as it turned out, was not enough. The company needed extra workers. That, in light of its employment policy, would take time. The division manager of the Advanced Packages Division had to ask the production manager for three more workers; he in turn had to see if he could find them elsewhere in the company. Only when he couldn't were new ones able to be hired. As the Western Electric deadline approached, all the workers had to put in a lot of overtime. They did this in Japanese style—"I don't mind working overtime because I want to help the division ship a lot of parts," one said—but it was too late. Only 25 percent of the Western Electric order arrived on time, just barely enough to keep the account.

A purely American company, one suspects, would have handled the crisis somewhat differently. A big order like Western Electric's might have entailed hiring many new workers, who would then be laid off when the order was completed. Failure to meet the order deadline could have led to reorganization of the responsible departments. Consultants might have been called in to analyze the problem, or a topflight manager from another part of the company brought in to "straighten things out." Discipline might have been tightened up, with recalcitrant workers fired or transferred.

At Kyocera the response to the company's failure was another compa. The production department had lost face—but the sales department, again helped out by a little sake and a relaxed atmosphere, smoothed things over. Managers and salespeople discussed the problem, joked with each other, and reestablished the feeling of a family that was so important to Kyocera's operations. Six weeks later the group caught up on the Western Electric order.

"I GET the impression," a Japanese visitor to the United States told Harvard's Robert Hayes, "that American managers spend more time worrying about the well-being and loyalty of their stockholders, whom they don't know, than they do about their workers, whom they do know. This is very puzzling. The Japanese manager is always asking himself how he can share the company's success with his workers." The difference in attitude suggested by this remark is undeniable. Yet Hayes, for one, thinks that the Japanese approach is not as foreign to Americans as it sometimes seems. Americans, he notes, "love to work on smoothly functioning teams." Moreover, the " 'we're all in this together' attitude of Japanese companies is . . . reminiscent of the American management tradition of 'let's roll up our sleeves and get it done.' " Even lifetime employment isn't unheard of: "In most large U.S. companies," Hayes writes, "30% to 40% of the work force has lifetime employment, in the sense that any production worker who has worked for more than 10 years is almost never laid off."

Few U.S. firms, however, have cultivated the sense of cooperation and mutual commitment that characterizes the Japanese enterprise. Isolated experiments here have shown that this kind of attitude can be encouraged, often with beneficial results, and the experience of firms like Kyocera suggests that some aspects of the Japanese style can be imported, albeit with some difficulty. What remains to be seen is whether the U.S. economy's current troubles encourage American managers to experiment more with ways of involving workers in their firms' operations—or whether, in contrast, hard times lead only to retrenchment, caution, and a business-as-usual approach.

In the context of this book, the "Japanese economic miracle" has an obvious but significant lesson. There is little evidence to suggest that the Japanese are better than Americans at developing new products or at marketing them. Their industries need as much capital as ours and face the same kind of competitive pressure. But the Japanese do seem to have a fundamentally different way of working together, and in some respects a different attitude toward enterprise itself. Insofar as these factors account for Japan's economic success, they suggest an important truth about today's business: namely, that the nature of human relations at the shop-floor level may, in the 1980s, be one of the most critical problems business has to face.

THROUGHOUT THIS BOOK we have been examining the tasks that face an entrepreneur or a company in getting its business off the ground. These tasks—ranging from finance to marketing to taking on the competition—are like a series of obstacles to be overcome. When they are not overcome, a company fails.

Corporate failure is not quite the same thing as individual failure. Ambrose Bierce once characterized a corporation as "an ingenious device for obtaining individual profit without individual responsibility." And it is true that, thanks to the principle of limited liability, a company's managers can no longer be hauled into debtor's prison when the firm goes bankrupt. Nor, of course, can their personal assets be touched.

Still, the failure of an enterprise can be a traumatic event. For the managers involved, failure invariably means a protracted period of hard work and intense pressure, followed by gnawing feelings of personal inadequacy. Others, such as a failed company's workers, may find themselves hurt and angry yet utterly powerless to affect their situation. A failure that is large enough can have devastating effects on a community or region.

Some of the reasons for a company's failure can be found outside the firm, in a slumping economy or aggressive competition. Some can usually be found inside the firm, in management errors. In this sense the roots of failure are always different, for human beings can be wonderfully resourceful in finding new ways to make mistakes. As the next chapter shows, these mistakes can be plain enough in retrospect. At the time, however, they are simply maneuvers or strategies that any of us might have chosen to pursue. The fact that they turned out wrong indicates only that business, like most human activities, is not a sure thing.

9. Failure

ROUTE SIGNS along most of the beltway circling Greater Boston now say I-95 in deference to the Interstate Highway System of which the road has become a part. But local residents still call it Route 128, remembering its previous designation. What they mean, as often as not, is not just a highway but an industry.

Like California's Silicon Valley, Route 128 was a birthplace of the computer revolution. Staffed by scientists and engineers from Harvard, M.I.T., and the area's other universities, computer companies sprang up like mushrooms. Drivers on 128 grew accustomed to seeing new buildings appear almost every month on the undeveloped, accessible land around the highway.

Frequently these buildings bore unfamiliar names, for like all growing industries the computer business was spawning new companies at an alarming rate. Established firms provided a training ground for young engineers who then, armed with a new invention or idea, went out on their own. Thus IBM subsidized the future directors of Digital Equipment Corporation (DEC), now a $3.5-billion company that dominates the minicomputer market. DEC, in turn, gave birth to both Data General Corp. and Data Terminal Corp. Data General—the company profiled in Tracy Kidder's best-selling book *The Soul of a New Machine*—has turned out to be one of DEC's top competitors.

IN 1957 a man named Tom Horgan started work with IBM, and in 1960 he became manager of its Graphics and Display Development Division. During his eight-year tenure there, Horgan came up with a brilliant new system for entering data into a computer. IBM's system at the time used the punch cards that were known to one and all as "IBM cards." Horgan's system, which would later be called the IKE, dispensed with the cards. Instead it allowed the key operator to type up data that appeared on a televisionlike screen and then entered the computer electronically. Because operators could see what they were typing, the system was cheaper, faster, and more accurate than IBM's.

IBM didn't buy the idea. The reason was simple enough: the company couldn't produce the IKE without rendering all its own systems obsolete. So Horgan took his invention and several other people and set out to form his own company. Bruce Elmblad, a West Point classmate of Horgan's, raised venture capital from J.H. Whitney and J.A. Walker. In March 1968 the team launched Inforex, Inc., on Route 128.

A year and a half later the IKE appeared. It swept the market. Back then, the IKE's packaged tape and disc drives were state-of-the-art technology. The product cut deeply into IBM's territory—and best of all, competitors weren't even on the horizon. By 1971 there were 700 IKE's in operation. Inforex stock, which had averaged $22.50 a share in 1971, shot up first to $38 and then to $48. When the company issued 500,000 new shares in 1972, 490,000 of them were snapped up immediately.

Early employees grew rich overnight. Bruce Elmblad recalls, for example, how Jerry Gray, an Inforex technician, drove to work one day in a shiny new Corvette. When asked how he could afford such an expensive car, Gray replied, "It only cost me $23.30— that's what I paid for the stock I sold to buy the car." Unlike Gray, the company's top managers held onto their stock rather than cash any of it in. And why not? The future seemed rosy, and in all likelihood the stock would continue its climb.

In fact exactly the opposite happened. Without anyone knowing it, Inforex hit its peak in 1972. Seven years later the founders would be gone. In their place a man named Jerry Jones would be trying to salvage what was left of the company with a last, desperate act.

On October 25, 1979, Inforex, under Jones, the new president, filed for reorganization in U.S. Bankruptcy Court.

IF RISK is the element underlying business enterprise, then businesses by definition run the risk of failure. In fact many thousands of businesses do fail every year, leaving unpaid debts totaling in the billions. The rate mounts, not surprisingly, whenever the economy enters a recession. In the first two months of 1982, for example, 4,846 businesses collapsed, including 1,800 companies with liabilities greater than $100,000. The failure rate had increased nearly 100 percent over the previous year's in the country's most troubled regions, about 30 percent overall. According to Dun & Bradstreet, the failure rate for early 1982 was 80 per 10,000 companies—not far from the 1933 rate of 100 per 10,000.

Failure, of course, can take many forms. "Four-fifths of all bankruptcy filings," reports the *Wall Street Journal*, "are for straight liquidations, in which a company's assets are scattered at auctions and its jobs lost altogether." The more complex of these liquidations typically involve a lengthy period of receivership, in which a court-appointed trustee oversees the dissolution of a company and the settlement of its debts. The largest and most spectacular failures sometimes lead to some kind of government rescue. Rolls-Royce, for example, nearly went broke in the early 1970s when auditors discovered it couldn't pay the penalties it owed Lockheed for failing to produce an aircraft engine on schedule. Unwilling to let Rolls sink, the British government nationalized the firm. Similarly, when the Penn Central collapsed, the U.S. government arranged for many of its assets to be taken over by the two quasipublic railroad corporations ConRail and Amtrak. Two other big companies—Lockheed and Chrysler—avoided bankruptcy in recent years only because the government bailed them out with loan guarantees and other forms of assistance. The DeLorean Motor Company, as described in Chapter Four, went into receivership only because the British government finally refused to provide additional assistance.

Not all busines failures, though, lead to closed doors or government bailouts. A company that is failing may take a step known as filing for reorganization under Chapter XI of the Federal Bankruptcy Act. The law spells out a series of procedures through which the company's managers and its creditors attempt to agree on a plan for reorganizing the firm, restructuring its debt, and getting it back in business. The logic behind the law is simple enough: sometimes companies get themselves in trouble through management errors or other problems that can be rectified. "Many companies have survived Chapter XI and done remarkably well once they got out," says Judge Thomas Lawless of Boston's U.S. Bankruptcy Court. "It's like getting a virus. You feel bad, but there's no sense saying, 'Well, let's blow the fellow's head off.' You feel, maybe it's better to give them a chance." The *Wall Street Journal* describes Chapter XI's function in equally graphic terms: "It . . . helps prevent secured creditors from feasting on a debtor's assets and leaving a carcass with little long-term hope for survival."

The law was not always so accommodating to enterprises in trouble. In the mid-nineteenth century, creditors could destroy a company at the first sign of an unpaid bill by going to court and forcing the firm into bankruptcy. During the panics of that era, thousands of temporarily insolvent businesses were stripped bare by nervous creditors—and when those companies went down, they took many others with them, thereby escalating the panic. Eventually pressure began to mount for a uniform bankruptcy law that would give businesses a chance to stay in business while they tried to settle their debts in an equitable manner and put their operations back on their feet.

The first such law, the Federal Bankruptcy Act of

1867, did that, though it was often criticized for its partiality toward creditors. Its successor, the Federal Bankruptcy Act of 1979, is sometimes thought to be unfairly slanted toward debtors. In 1980, for example, U.S. bankruptcy courts redistributed some $70 billion in liabilities and $40 billion in debtor assets, leaving creditors with a net loss of $30 billion. Chapter XI filings, which previously accounted for only 12 percent of business bankruptcies, jumped to 20 percent of the total only a year after the act was passed.

Whatever the reason, attitudes toward bankruptcy have been changing. "Fifteen years ago when I became a judge," observed Roy Babbitt of the U.S. Bankruptcy Court for the Southern District of New York, "bankruptcy was something to avoid at all costs. Those of us who grew up during the Depression know the necessity of paying off debts. That attitude would appear to exist no longer in America." And there are, of course, those who welcome the recent rash of filings, notably the law and accounting firms that specialize in managing such cases. One little known provision of the 1979 law eliminated what the *Wall Street Journal* described as "a longstanding requirement that a 'spirit of economy' prevail when bankruptcy lawyers set their fees." As a result, said the *Journal*, the "big, rich law firms" that handle bankruptcies are getting "even bigger and richer."

In the volatile and fast-growing computer business, failure is a fact of life. It can hit both large and small companies, and it doesn't seem to depend much, so far, on general economic conditions or on the varying provisions of federal law. Rather, failure awaits the company that fails to develop exactly what the market wants when it wants it—and that fails to follow its first act with a second and a third that are equally successful.

The most famous story of failure in the industry does not involve a bankrupt company, but it does illustrate the pitfalls that await even the biggest firm. Robert Sarnoff, chief executive officer of RCA and son of electronics pioneer David Sarnoff, wanted to make his mark in computers as his father had in color television, by catapulting RCA to the forefront of the market. That meant challenging IBM, and Sarnoff knew it would not be an easy task. In 1970, when RCA was making its move, the company's sales topped $3 billion, ranking it among the nation's largest twenty-five corporations. But IBM, with $7.5 billion in computer revenue alone, was almost six times as large as its nearest competitor.

Undeterred by the obstacles, Sarnoff launched "Project Intercept." The project's mission, as its name suggests, was to cut into IBM's market with a new line of computers. The machines needed to have a modest price tag in order to win customers. Since his engineers had told him that a completely new line couldn't be ready before 1972, Sarnoff decided to revamp the firm's existing Spectra line, modifying the body and souping up the memory bank. He offered customers an extra incentive to buy the machines too. RCA would convert their IBM equipment, the company promised, and pay a penalty if the RCA machines failed.

To head RCA's computer effort, Sarnoff had hired L. Edwin Donegan, a former IBM employee who, within a year at RCA, rose to vice-president and general manager. Donegan, with almost missionary zeal, patterned the new division almost exactly after

IBM. He staffed it with former IBM employees, despite the fact that their aggressive, competitive tactics didn't always sit well with RCA's staid management. He even modeled his products after IBM's. Project Intercept planned its own machines on the basis of a detailed study of IBM's 370 line.

Two of IBM's computers—the 370/155 and the 370/165—had been announced when RCA unveiled its own models, and they carried few surprises. Some weeks thereafter, however, IBM introduced a new model, the 145. That turned out to be a completely new machine, with a larger memory bank and a lower price than RCA had counted on. To counter, Donegan pirated yet more IBM engineers. He also staffed 27 of his 34 marketing divisions with new regional managers, all schooled in IBM accounting practices.

Finance and pricing were both problems. As W. David Gardner explains in the book *Great Business Disasters,* "It is one of the great ironies of the computer industry that the better you do, the worse off you can be financially. Because the industry is largely a lease and rental business, companies that grow rapidly—and RCA was one—are required to make massive capital outlays, but since the equipment is leased, they must wait long periods to get their money back." Early in 1971 RCA's operating earnings fell, forcing it to resort to long-term financing. In May IBM cut the price of the specialized equipment known as peripherals. That put IBM's line lower than RCA's, and customers flocked back.

On September 17, 1971, RCA pulled out of the computer business. The move had severe repercussions: 8,000 employees lost their jobs and 500 customers were left holding a billion dollars' worth of

RCA equipment. But the $490 million loss, which outranked the Edsel as America's greatest business disaster, became a pre-tax write-off for the huge corporation. And the news that RCA was pulling out of computers drove its stock up for the first time in months.

The success story in computers—after IBM, anyway—is usually thought to be Apple, a company that has become virtually a household name only a few years after its inception. But even that story illustrates the possibility of failure. In 1976 Steven Jobs and Stephen Wozniak, two Berkeley dropouts, raised $1,300 to start a makeshift production line. Their invention was an easy-to-use personal computer that proved to be one of the industry's biggest sellers. Jobs and Wozniak also wrote a clear instruction manual for consumers, making the Apple seem both accessible and familiar. The results, of course, were astonishing. Since 1976 Apple has sold some 250,000 personal computers, hitting as many as 20,000 a month. Sales soared from $2.7 million in 1977 to $300 million in 1981.

Yet Apple faced problems as early as 1980. A second-generation machine, the Apple III, had to be temporarily withdrawn from the market so its technical bugs could be fixed. And competitors were coming up fast. While Apple controlled nearly a quarter of the personal computer market, Tandy Corporation's Radio Shack model had pulled even in sales, and IBM itself introduced a personal computer. Apple in turn upped its expenditures on research and development and tightened its control over manufacturing costs in an attempt to keep prices down. But it learned that instant success does not guarantee longevity in the computer business.

Daniel H. Fylstra, chairman of Personal Software, Inc., thinks Jobs and Wozniak were lucky: "If an Apple came along today, I don't think it would stand a chance." A study of computer industry failures by the University of Santa Clara professor Albert Bruno bears out Fylstra's assessment. Though almost all the companies in California's Silicon Valley survive their first four years, Bruno found, about a quarter of them collapse in the second four. Promising products are sabotaged by managerial mistakes. And the larger the company, the slimmer the chance that its products will continue to be on target.

IN THE SPRING of 1979 Inforex adopted a rainbow as the company's new logo. The colorful arc turned up everywhere. A slide show proclaimed 1979 as "the greatest year in our 10-year history." Six months later the company filed for protection under Chapter XI of the Federal Bankruptcy Act.

The causes of this failure are as complex as the bankruptcy proceedings that were supposed to resolve it. Industry analysts cite Inforex's inability to come up with a successful second product as the chief reason for the company's demise. But nearly all computer firms experience similar dry spells. Inforex's trouble lay deeper—in the company's markets, in its management, and in its failure to make the transition from an entrepreneurial corporation to a managerial one.

By 1972 Inforex was facing the problem Apple had to face: competition. Entrex and Mohawk Data both had versions of the IKE that could do everything the original could do, and often faster. Entrex in particular, with a larger-capacity machine than the IKE, managed to cut into Inforex's base of customers just as Inforex itself had sliced into IBM's. Worse, Inforex still hadn't come up with a profitable second product. Technical bugs, materials shortages, and delays in delivery plagued all its new production lines. The board of directors forced out Tom Horgan, replacing him with another West Point graduate named Tim Cronin. Just as RCA's Donegan had overstaffed his division with IBM, so Cronin stuck mainly to West Point or Annapolis graduates. But instead of falling into rank, say industry analysts, Inforex's top management team was rife with dissension, especially over the issue of growth. Ignoring warnings from chief financial officer Bob Moore, Cronin continued to expand the company's operations without selling enough stock to finance the expansion. Like RCA, Inforex was living on borrowed money.

In October 1974 the company borrowed an additional $13 million from three banks. One, the First National Bank of Boston, stipulated that Inforex sell more stock. In complying with that stipulation, however, Inforex unwittingly dug itself even deeper into a hole. Because of a change in the Accountancy Principles Act of 1971, Inforex and many other lease-income companies were about to be pummeled on the stock market. Before, income from a leased piece of equipment could be counted on the books as a sale. So when Inforex leased $1 million worth of equipment to a customer, it could record $1 million in income, even if only, say, $100,000 was trickling in each month. The change in accounting procedures put an end to this practice, and for good reason. Corporate reports boasting of millions of dollars in sales kept Wall Street interested and stock prices high, but they didn't accurately reflect a company's

performance. No one would know from Inforex's
1974 annual report, for example, that the company
was in fact suffering a serious cash-flow crisis that
would eventually cripple its operations.

There were other problems too. Chief among them
was Inforex's failure in product development. Between 1974 and 1979 it had spent millions on R & D
and start-up costs, including $15 million on its Model
7000 File-Management System alone. The trouble
was that its products bore too little relationship to
each other. The 7000 was used primarily for track-
ing receipts. The System 3300 was for labor data
and the System 5000 for inventories. "Inforex had
nine unrelated systems serving various areas of
manufacturing," said manufacturing division manager Gil Gilbert in March 1979. "They were unrelated because each was developed independently."

The contrast between Inforex and a company that
Inforex had once tried to buy was striking. Datapoint
Corporaion, a $500-million San Antonio–based manu-
facturer of office computer equipment, suffered similar product-development problems. In the late 1960s
Datapoint's chief product was highly specialized
computer terminals with a narrow base of potential
customers. Its next product, though, was a self-
contained, all-purpose office computer. That broad-
ened its base of customers, and sales began to soar.
Inforex, by contrast, ran into the problem pinpointed
by a Datapoint engineer discussing his company's
product strategy. "The reason for the high failure
rate in this industry," he said, "is that the technology is so radically new that it's hard to test your
market. In many cases the market doesn't even exist
yet." Inforex couldn't be sure its machines were

even needed, let alone that customers would buy them.

Another of Inforex's problems could be traced to marketing failure. The company's new 7000 line—a machine designed to hold, process, and retrieve data from an auxiliary computer—had been plagued by delivery delays. Partly as a result, the sales force had been concentrating on leasing upgraded equipment to old customers instead of seeking out new customers who would buy new equipment. In 1978 Inforex's goal for new equipment leases was 120, of which it made only 60. Its goal for upgraded equipment was 30 units; it leased 90.

This strategy proved costly. Customers paying, say, $800 a month for old equipment might be asked to pay an additional $200 a month to update their systems. That raised the monthly rental to $1,000—but Inforex's cost to upgrade the system was nearer to $14,000, a fact not known to company executives until much later. Meanwhile the company wasn't selling enough new equipment, and a lot of old equipment lay idle in the factories, awaiting upgrading. Like RCA, Inforex sank deeper into the red.

While all these problems were being confronted, Inforex's top executives held onto their stock, refusing to sell out. Paul L. Dobbins, a New York financial analyst, recalls the problem exactly. "I think the original Inforex founders always looked through rose-tinted glasses," he says. "They never sold their stock. When it went up to $48, I begged Tom Horgan to take out even 25 percent of his position. At that time, around 1973, he had over 100,000 shares worth $5 million. If he only sold 10 percent, he'd have half a million in hard, firm cash. But so many Inforex executives held on till the end, riding it all the way down."

Inforex itself held on for a while, but an unmistakable sign of a crunch came in 1978. Posting its second quarterly loss in the third quarter of 1978, Inforex found itself in violation of agreements covering $9 million in loans. The banks, which had required the firm to post a profit every quarter, forced Inforex to renegotiate its loans. New loans brought higher interest rates, and the company was already in debt well over its apparent capacity to pay. The fact was not lost on Wall Street: the stock that had once soared to $48.00 a share now crashed to $4.75.

In the spring of 1979 Inforex's debts came to $60 million. Jerry E. Jones, a lawyer-turned-executive who had been with the company only two years, succeeded Cronin. Jones slashed the payroll and trimmed the budget. By late fall, though, the firm was unable to meet its $1 million semiannual interest payment on its $20 million in loans. In response to its October 25 bankruptcy petition, Judge Lawless of the U.S. Bankruptcy Court in Boston granted the company protection from its creditors. Under the court's terms, Inforex was allowed to spend $2 million of incoming cash every week, but not profits from future contracts. It had to cancel a recently negotiated $7.9 million contract with the Army for the installation of 62 data processing systems. And it had to come up with a viable plan for paying off its debts by April 1, 1980, the date of its hearing.

UNDER CHAPTER XI, Inforex had a good shot at being saved. A 1979 Brookings Institution report found that one-third of all businesses that file for bankruptcy under Chapter XI survive. Some of the reasons are explained by Sidney Rutberg in his study of bankruptcy, *Ten Cents on the Dollar*. "Under Chapter XI," writes Rutberg, "it's possible for an insolvent company to work down its debts through an arrangement that only a bare majority of its creditors accept, have its solvency restored through debt reduction, avoid paying taxes on the profit earned from forgiven debt, issue stock without the necessity of SEC [Securities and Exchange Commission] registration and get out from under burdensome leases or other long-term contracts. All this can be done without giving up control of the business to a court-appointed trustee as would occur in Chapter X."

In fact many a black bankruptcy cloud has had its silver lining, for just the reasons Rutberg outlines. The White Motor Company, for example—a Michigan-based manufacturer of heavy trucks and farm equipment—came through Chapter XI with a weakened but intact organization. White had lost $104 million in the 1974–75 recession and couldn't seem to get back on its feet. Like Inforex it found itself cash poor and heavily dependent on its 27 banks for working capital. On September 4, 1979, the company filed under Chapter XI. It was some $1.2 billion in debt.

Early in 1980 a new management team led by Cruse Moss and Keith Mazurek began to cut costs. They laid off two layers of upper management, saving some $8 million, and cut the number of white-collar workers by 35 percent. They reorganized plants, closing one truck-group office and stopping heavy-truck production in another. For a while the outcome was uncertain. Just as White's management hadn't figured on interest rates over 20 percent, it also hadn't foreseen the collapse of the heavy-truck market in 1980. Of the 65,000 units the industry was scheduled to produce that year, 44,000 had to be canceled.

In the end, though, White survived. Temporarily relieved of $300 million in interest and liability payments, White was able to use current assets plus income to pay employees and suppliers. Volvo, the Swedish auto manufacturer, absorbed the company's money-losing heavy-truck operations along with its financing subsidiary, leaving the organization smaller but stronger. Moss observed, "The situation provides the two ingredients that had been missing— time and money—for the new management to complete the restructuring of the company."

Chapter XI proceedings typically average a year and a half from filing to settlement. They are seldom smooth. Before the filing, nervous creditors may already have begun to pressure the company and jockey for position, generating ill will all around. Shortly before Braniff's bankruptcy, for instance, word got out that the airline had secured its biggest lenders' loans by mortgaging its newest and most valuable airplanes. Later, according to the *Wall Street Journal*, "Braniff apparently tried to mollify the critics by mortgaging the rest of its equipment to secure debt." Still, the 23 banks and 14 insurance companies that held Braniff's debt were prone to dissension, notably over a Braniff proposal that the creditors swap their loans for the airline's stock. "Disagreements over the size and form of the swap practically assure substantial changes in Braniff's current proposal," the *Journal* reported at the time.

After filing for protection, a company must meet with all its secured creditors. At this meeting, usually six months after filing, creditors and lawyers accept or reject a debtor's proposed repayment schedule and plan for restructuring. While under Chapter XI a debtor must propose to pay off the total amount of valid debts, creditors will only back a plan they think the company can actually honor. To finance the plan, a debtor must first make a cash deposit for administrative expenses and primary debts. These alone cost Inforex $2 million. It can then raise additional money by selling off assets—real estate, vehicles, and so on—not necessary to the business. In most cases, though, companies must raise new capital during Chapter XI proceedings. This is an acid test: a firm able to raise capital while under Chapter XI is one that creditors are usually willing to take a chance on.

Like White's management, Jones cut Inforex's costs dramatically. Firing the company's previous executive board, he staffed it with top computer people, none of whom were West Point men. And he reduced the payroll from 1,200 to 280. "We were called into a meeting," a former Inforex employee recalls. "Those who were called in were told they were staying. Those who weren't were laid off." Switchboard operators were given new lists of employees, less than half the original length. "There were whole families laid off," an operator remembers. "You'd see the list and feel sick." Laid-off employees ran to the bank to cash their checks, some of which bounced. It was not a happy time for the company or for its workers.

Nor did things go much better over the next few months.

*   *   *

WHEN JERRY JONES traveled to a downtown Boston bank on April 1, 1980, to meet his creditors, he had run out of both time and money. "We're very, very tired," he said. "It's partly the trauma, the uncertainty of the situation. You end up needing some good news, some breakthrough." For 60 days none had come. Now Inforex's creditors, he feared, would be calling the shots, and there was little doubt as to what they were looking for. "The basic goal," explained Bob Truslow of the Industrial National Bank, "is to get as much money out of it as you can."

The creditors did have a dilemma of their own. Which would raise them more money, liquidating the business or trying to get it back on its feet? "The risk for the creditor," explained Robert Gargill, an attorney for the Wells Fargo Bank, "is properly evaluating whether or not a debtor can fulfill his financial promises." Their careers too turned on the right decision. At Inforex's hearing the banks stood to lose some $30 million, including $2.3 million owed to Manufacturers Hanover Trust, $3 million to Wells Fargo, $8 million to First National Bank of Chicago, and a whopping $17 million to Lease Financing Corporation. Not all the creditors moreover, had identical interests. In the strongest position were creditors based in the East: their collateral, mostly in the form of newer IKE's, could easily be converted into cash through local leasing. Creditors like Wells Fargo, whose collateral was older IKE's spread out all over the country, were in a weaker position. Yet if just one creditor refused to accept Inforex's repayment plan, no agreement would be reached and the company would be liquidated.

To the inevitable bargaining between creditor and debtor, then, would be added bargaining and dealing among creditors themselves. John Manaras, Inforex's vice-president, outlined the strategy both sides would be following as the meeting began. "The posturing, the negotiation, the staking out of position is the most important part of the whole," he explained. "Sometimes we characterize it as a dance: not giving up too much too early. Letting the other guy make the first move. You have to stake out the maximum amount of territory so that you're not perceived as giving up anything even though you intend to give up a lot."

After three grueling hours of questioning, the Inforex team left to let the bankers fight it out. They, in turn, wrestled for two days. Finally the last one fell into line and accepted Inforex's plan. Over the next six years, in addition to its $2.6 million cash deposits, Inforex would pay its creditors $40 million. The company, Jones thought, could get back to work.

But not, as it turned out, for long. Unlike some firms, Inforex had no successful line of products to fall back on, and not even a bankruptcy agreement could solve that problem. On June 11, barely two months after the agreement, Inforex reported its previous fourth-quarter loss at $23.9 million on revenues of $14.3 million. The company was ripe for sale. Bids from McDonnell-Douglas and Four-Phase Company fell far short of what it needed. But a bid from Datapoint, the Texas company that Inforex had once tried to buy, did not. Datapoint offered Inforex shareholders market value for their stock, then totaling around $6.4 million. It also agreed to assume all of Inforex's outstanding debts.

Inforex accepted Datapoint's offer. On August 28 creditors and the court approved the sale, and on September 23 Inforex was discharged from all debts secured under Chapter XI. Six days later John L. Hale, a Datapoint vice-president in charge of field operations for customer service, was appointed Inforex's new president. Jones, like all the company's executives, was let go as part of the deal. He was fatalistic about it. "I'm not the first to go through the withdrawal," he said the night it happened. "I don't have the power, the control I had this morning. They'll be nice to me, but I'm not any longer important in the scheme of things."

Hale eventually whipped Inforex back into shape. He cut back on manufacturing space, scrapped the unprofitable 7000 line, and concentrated on IKE production. Datapoint's real interest, though, had been in Inforex's wholly owned European subsidiaries. These financially sound operations, accounting for between 60 and 70 percent of Inforex's sales, were exempt and therefore unscathed by the Chapter XI proceedings. A European distribution operation like Inforex's was just what Datapoint needed to expand its fast-growing operations. A side benefit of the deal was Inforex's 1,800 domestic customers, including some Fortune 500 companies, many of whom had long-term leases on video-display equipment. Along with these customers, Datapoint would also inherit a sizable field-maintenne force to service the 45,000 terminals Inforex had installed since 1970.

FREQUENTLY, the ultimate roots of corporate failure lie in larger economic troubles over which a company has no control. Airline deregulation was widely thought to be the chief cause of Braniff's failure and of the troubles experienced by many other carriers. Trucking deregulation caused a rash of bankruptcies among trucking firms. New competition can have the same effect, as evidenced by the damages wrought on U.S. auto companies by the Japanese. So, of course, can long-term changes in economic behavior. "Small oil and gas firms," said the *Wall Street Journal* in 1982, "are quickly dropping from sight as energy users mend their wasteful ways"—a development that makes the success of entrepreneurial endeavors like Bill Brodnax's Taurus Petroleum all the more remarkable.

But Datapoint's acquisition of Inforex underscores another fundamental lesson. Most often, the roots of corporate failure lie in poor management. A 1979 Dun & Bradstreet study found that 90 percent of business failures in that year could be traced to management error. In *Corporate Collapse: The Causes and Symptoms*, John Argenti defines poor management as "one-man rule, a nonparticipating board, unbalanced top team, lack of management depth, weak finance function, and combined chairman-chief executive." Inforex was guilty of almost all these sins. The company's incoherent product strategy, its lack of touch with its own sales force (once credited by industry experts as among the best in its field), and its poor financial information all suggest a management that was not on top of its own affairs.

Without coherent management, a company growing as fast as Inforex simply can't make the transition to an effective large-scale corporation. Mohawk Data, its competitor, did. So did Datapoint. Inforex didn't, as founder Tom Horgan readily acknowledges. "There are an awful lot of companies like Inforex that come up very fast," he says. "Somewhere around the $50- or $60- million transition period, they either blow apart or get through it and continue growing. We didn't get through that $50-million point in the smoothest or swiftest way we could."

Corporate failure does not necessarily bespeak individual failure. Many of the entrepreneurs in this book failed—but would not be labeled as failures. Bill Brodnax drilled 12 out of 13 dry holes in a single year, but his success lay in his ability to raise capital, keep on drilling, and eventually hit a producer. John Z. DeLorean's company went bankrupt, but for a while he seemed successful in his ability even to get the company started. Similarly, Inforex's legacy to Jerry Jones was a reputation for saving companies, a reputation that he converted into a position as a highly paid industry consultant. The vice-president, John Manaras, bounced back as an officer of another computer company.

The one man who warned of Inforex's trouble, financial officer Bob Moore, remained unemployed for some time. Moore, who lives near Boston and spent a long time looking for work around Route 128, was philosophical about his situation. "A president is in a very difficult position. If he picks a man who, despite his good credentials and experience, is tainted with failure, that president is responsible for him." He was also, surprisingly enough, philosophical about Inforex's sad story—though his voice was not without a trace of regret and self-blame. "When you think about the fact that here is a young, exploding industry fraught with glorious successes, you know it takes some kind of special talent to fail in the middle of that," he said. "And that's what we did. So what you have is the classic American tragedy. The classic American failure."

IN A WAY, Calvin Coolidge was right. The business of America is business.

Consider, for example, the plight of the young idealist who proposes to attend an anti-business rally in a downtown park. He sleeps the night before on a mattress made by a business called Sealy, in a house owned by businesses called landlords or banks. He rises to an alarm clock (Westclox), puts on his jeans (Levi Strauss), and sits down to breakfast (Kellogg's). He reads the news as packaged and served up by *The New York Times*, gets into a car built by General Motors or Toyota, drives along a street built by construction companies. At the rally he listens approvingly to denunciations of business. The words are amplified by loudspeaking equipment built by a business called Ace Electronics and rented from a business called Jones Rental Agency.

It is difficult, in our society, to live or breathe without somehow depending on business. This intimacy, however, has not always bred mutual affection and respect, as the familiar image of the young protester demonstrates. The fact is that Americans have always had an ambivalent attitude toward business. So indeed have people throughout history. When Jesus threw the money changers out of the temple, he was probably not the first to charge them with violating God's will.

In today's world this ambivalent attitude is reflected in a variety of controversies as to business's proper role in society. These issues—whether the pursuit of private profit can serve the public interest, how much government should aid or regulate business, and so on—are not ones that can easily be resolved once and for all. On the contrary, every generation must thrash them out anew and reach a resolution appropriate to its era. The final chapter looks at how successive generations have come to terms with some of them over the years—and how one company in particular has reflected a changing consensus about the respective roles that business and government should play in society. The epilogue reflects on changing conceptions of the fundamental purpose of business itself.

10. Business and Society

THE YEAR 1776 saw the publication of two documents that helped change the course of history. One, of course, was the Declaration of Independence, written principally by Thomas Jefferson. The other was Adam Smith's *The Wealth of Nations*.

Both Jefferson and Smith were liberals, even revolutionaries of sorts, for thier day. Both railed against arbitrary authority and preached the virtues of freedom and democracy. Both believed in the value of hard work and enterprise. Yet there was a critical difference between them. For Smith the moving force of society was the independent businessman seeking to make a profit. Guided by the market's invisible hand, the businessman served the community as a whole. Jefferson shared only part of this vision. He treasured the image of the self-sufficient yeoman farmer, but he felt a deep distrust of those he viewed as money-grubbing urban capitalists. The capitalists, of course, didn't like him much either. When Jefferson as president ordered an embargo on trade with Great Britain, the Northeastern states, heavily dependent on foreign trade, threatened to secede from the union.

As the nineteenth century progressed, it was Smith's vision more than Jefferson's that seemed to be guiding the nation's development. America and its business were both growing. So too was the Smithian notion that whatever business did would work out for the good of all—and that the businessman, therefore, was himself imbued with high moral purpose. Historian Sidney Fine describes the prevailing belief in these words.

> Production and distribution are best conducted by individuals in pursuit of their own interests. . . . This tendency of the individual to do what is best for himself leads to his doing that which is best for the community, since the community interest is but the aggregate of individual interests. . . . The mere money-getter, in advancing his own selfish desires, yet occasions an increase in the product and a reduction of the cost of life's necessities and thus brings better conditions to all.

The popular economist Edward Atkinson put it more succinctly in 1869: "The Lord maketh the selfishness of man to work for the material welfare of his kind." And Calvin Coolidge echoed the belief as late as the 1920s: "The man who builds a factory builds a temple," wrote Coolidge. "The man who works worships there."

Though business ultimately came to dominate much of American life, its moral ascendancy was never firmly established. Particularly as the century wore on, Jeffersonian themes began to reappear in the midst of the general celebration. The Populists and many others attacked "Wall Street" as a den not only of iniquity but also of narrow self-interest opposed to the national welfare. A nascent labor movement attacked industry for its lack of concern for the working man and woman. The sharpest debates focused on two related themes. One was the issue of bigness—monopoly—as symbolized by the trusts. The other was the question as to the proper role of government in the economy. Those who believed that business could not be relied on to look out for the public interest came eventually to put their faith in Washington. That faith in turn gave rise to the Progressive movement, to Wilson's New Freedom, and to the New Deal.

FOR MOST of America's first century, economic enterprises were surprisingly small. As late as 1860, notes the historian Elisha P. Douglass, manufacturing establishments employed an average of about 10 people, and companies with as many as 200 workers were rare. Most of these enterprises, moreover, operated along traditional lines. Production methods were simple, markets local. And business procedures, says Douglass, "had not been radically altered during the fifty years preceding the [Civil] war."

In the next four decades all these aspects of business underwent a transformation. The systematic application of technology to production dramatically increased output. The growth of railroads and a nationwide telegraph system made possible the coordination of activities and the distribution of goods on a national scale. The invention of modern business organization and practices—what the historian Alfred D. Chandler has termed the "visible hand" of management—made possible the effective control of large-scale enterprises. These developments contributed to a vast increase in the size of American businesses. In much of the economy the small local establishment was replaced by the industrial corporation. And the parochial economic horizons of Americans were replaced by an ambitious, expansive mood. Historians Oscar and Mary Handlin describe this mood and its connection with the new economy in their book *The Wealth of the American People.* "The contrivers and dreamers, the big talk-and-plan men ran on," write the Handlins; "the size of the prize justified the odds. The palpable magnitude of the market, nationwide, the fivefold rise in the flow of goods to consumers, kept everyone in motion—inventors and investors, salesmen and dealers. The objects the multitutdes desired did not dribble out in cupfuls from scattered local sources but surged forth in torrents from mighty factories flooding the whole country by the force of their resources for innovation, efficiency, and mass output."

Along with the increase in the scale and objectives of economic endeavor came an increase in competition. Some kinds of competition had always existed, to be sure. But the small-scale, gentlemanly competition of local enterprises geared to small markets had not prepared Americans for the winner-take-all competition of huge companies trying to dominate the same national or regional market. The railroads, as noted in Chapter Seven, were the first to feel the pinch. As prices fell under competitive pressure, railroad men scrambled to set up alliances and associations that could divide up the business and eliminate price-cutting. Managers in nearly every other big industry soon were aping the railroads. "Businessmen might chorus their conviction that competition was the benign regulator of the industrial order," writes Elisha Douglass, "but this was solely an intellectual reaction. Moves taken to suppress competition had always been responses as instinctive as the raising of an arm to ward off a blow." Most moves, however, foundered on a paradox. All the companies in a given industry might have a long-term interest in limiting competition and dividing up the marketplace. But any one company had a short-term interest in cutting its prices or doing whatever else was necessary to increase its own business. Most trade associations and would-be cartels did not have much in the way of sanctions at their disposal. When one company decided to bolt the alliance, there was little that could be done.

In 1882 John D. Rockefeller created a device that would not only forestall competition but allow him to take full advantage of the possibilities for profit afforded by the booming market. Under Rockefeller's direction the stockholders of his Standard Oil Company put the corporation in the hands of nine trustees, who ran it in complete secrecy. These trustees proceeded to buy up other oil companies, to the point where they had acquired most of the oil-refining capacity in the United States. Thus was born the Standard Oil Trust. It wasn't long before similar arrangements were put into effect in other industries. Where trusts didn't work out, mergers, holding companies, and other devices allowed the same kind of market control. Technology and modern management methods had made possible the rise of the big corporation. Now the pressures of competition seemed to be creating giants.

The reaction, of course, was not long in coming. "Small, excluded competitors and consumers," write the Handlins, "ran screaming to the state for redress, reviving the old battle cries of the tea party and of Jackson's war against the monster bank. Monopoly! Popular opinion frowned upon the bullying Goliaths, particularly when the visible result was the concentration in a few hands of great fortunes lavishly thrown away in orgiastic living, while the virtuous little man lost all." In 1890 the Sherman Antitrust Act outlawed such schemes. Henceforth any collusion or contract designed to restrict competition or create a monopoly would be illegal. In the years after its passage the government intervened against many of the giants: the breakup of Standard Oil, for example, was finally upheld by the Supreme Court in 1911. Yet the question of what constitutes a monopoly—and the issue of how big is too big— was one that theoreticians, editorialists, and lawyers for both sides never did really resolve. The only thing certain was that it was now indisputably on the public agenda.

The issue of the proper role of government in the economy has never entirely been resolved either. In the early part of the nineteenth century, government was frequently seen simply as a partner for private enterprise. Its job was to do whatever was necessary to stimulate commerce and industry, even to the point of undertaking massive public works. "We hold it to be wisest," read the 1838 Whig party platform in New York State ". . . to apply the means of the state boldly and liberally to aid those great public works of railroads and canals which are beyond the means of unassisted private enterprise." The chief justice of the Pennsylvania Supreme Court, writing in 1853, went even further. "It is a grave error to suppose that the duty of the state stops with the establishment of those institutions which are necessary to the existence of government: such as those for the administration of justice, preservation of peace, and the protection of the country from foreign enemies," he wrote. "To aid, encourage, and stimulate commerce, domestic and foreign, is a duty of the sovereign as plain and universally recognized as any other."

Later in the century the doctrine of laissez faire gained in popularity, and the government was expected simply to keep its hands off business. There were, to be sure, some chinks in the doctrine's armor that had to be patched up with compromise. The antitrust act itself was one such compromise, though in fact it can easily be viewed as a way of protecting free enterprise and forestalling government regulation. Another was the Interstate Commerce Act (1887), which set up an agency to regulate competition among the railroads. But by the twentieth century a succession of Republican presidents (interrupted only by Woodrow Wilson) were ruling comfortably over a nation seemingly persuaded that the interests of business and the interests of the public were remarkably similar. "Never before," the *Wall Street Journal* marveled in 1925, "here or anywhere else, has a government been so completely fused with business." Andrew Mellon, Coolidge's secretary of the treasury, completed the equation. "The government," he said, "is just a business, and can and should be run on business principles."

The end of this subservience of government to

business came of course with the Crash of 1929 and the Depression that followed. Not that attitudes changed overnight. Henry Ford still insisted that government should "stick to the strict functioning of governing" and "let business alone." President Hoover, as the historian Arthur Schlesinger, Jr., points out, was depending on individuals, local initiatives, and mutual self-help—anything but the federal government—to relieve America of its miseries. The tide of the New Deal, however, soon swept over those who wanted to leave the principles of laissez faire alone. The National Industrial Recovery Act and later the National Labor Relations Act set minimum wages and maximum hours. The Social Security Act established government's responsibility for the welfare of those who were not working. And a host of agencies, from the Securities and Exchange Commission to the Federal Communications Commission were charged with overseeing specific sectors of the economy and preventing the abuses of laissez faire.

The trend of growing government intervention in the economy persisted in the decades that followed World War II. The growth in military spending and in transfer payments like Social Security meant that the government was now responsible for apportioning a sizable share of the national income. It was also asked, particularly in the 1960s and early 1970s, to regulate more and more aspects of the economy directly. Thus agencies like the Environmental Protection Agency, the Occupational Safety and Health Administration, and the Equal Employment Opportunity Commission came into being, each responsible for regulating the economy's behavior in a given area. The "Reagan revolution" of the 1980s promised to end the trend toward bigger and bigger government, but it was unlikely to undo most of what had been done already. In fact it can be seen simply as one more example of the continuing debate about government's role in the economy, a debate that has been part of American politics for a century and a half.

ALL THESE ISSUES—economic concentration, monopoly versus competition, the role of government regulation—seem to converge in the amazing story of the American Telephone and Telegraph Company. It is a company that has managed, through deft turns of policy and philosophy, to adapt itself to the peculiarly American visions of business that emerged in various periods over the years.

The Bell Telephone Company was founded in July 1877. A few months before, Alexander Graham Bell had placed the famous call to his assistant demonstrating his invention and had beaten his chief rival, Elisha Gray, to the patent office with a design of the new device. Armed with this patent, two of Bell's backers established the firm that bore the inventor's name. By autumn the Bell company had 600 subscribers.

The first two years were hard ones. The fledgling company nearly ran out of money, and Western Union, the giant of telegraphy, was actively trying to develop its own telephone system. But Bell beat down Western Union with a patent infringement suit, and by November 1881 it had a legal monopoly on telephone service. The company's annual report that year showed a modest-sized but well-established firm. American Bell, as it was then called, had earnings of $200,000. It had put 132,692 telephones into the hands of subscribers, and had set up exchanges in nearly every medium-sized and big city. In the next few years profits boomed. In 1882 the company made $500,000, in 1883 $750,000. By 1892 it had paid out $25 million in dividends.

The Yankee capitalists who ran American Bell in those days held a view of business and monopoly that wouldn't have shocked John D. Rockefeller a bit. Making the most of the advantage afforded them by their patent, they seemed to care little for either their public image or the public interest. When criticisms of Bell's rates began to surface, the company's president, William Forbes, responded haughtily, "The complaints as to rates are often made thoughtlessly, and in ignorance of the expenses and risks which attend the business." When the state of Indiana in 1885 passed a law regulating rates (a law that was later repealed), Forbes attacked the whole principle behind it. "Why should the telephone business be regulated as to price more than other industries?" he asked. "Sound public policy is surely against the regulation of the price of any class of commodities by law."

Forbes was expressing, of course, no more than the prevalent belief of the time, namely that a corporation's sole obligation was to its stockholders. If the public interest was served by the making of profits, so much the better—but profits came first. In Forbes's view, says John Brooks in his seminal study *Telephone*, "American Bell was merely doing in the telephone business through patent law what the oil and steel industries were doing through the formation of giant trusts. In places where government meddling, or unfavorable economic or technical conditions, made the prospects for profitable telephone service poor, American Bell's recourse was simply to refuse to extend service, or even to discontinue existing service."

The real father of the phone company, in any event, was not Forbes but Theodore N. Vail. Vail had first gone to work for American Bell in 1878, and in 1885 he was appointed president of the newly formed American Telephone and Telegraph Company, a subsidiary of American Bell set up to provide long-distance telephone service. Bell's patents, Vail knew, would expire in 1893. His job was to make the company strong enough, in the time it had left as a monopoly, to weather the storm of competition that would break when the patents expired.

To that end Vail did three things. First, he arranged for Bell to buy a controlling interest in the Western Electric Company, the country's largest electrical manufacturing firm. That would give Bell a strong source of supply under its own control. Second, he created New York–based AT&T, the subsidiary of which he then became president. Third, he set up a series of local telephone companies largely controlled by Bell. Vail's agents would urge local promoters to set up a firm and sell stock in it. In return for between 30 and 50 percent of the stock, Bell would grant the company a license to operate under its patent. Vail resigned in 1887 over differences with his employers, who did not share his long-term perspective. But by then the structure—a parent company, a wholly owned manufacturing arm, and a national network of operating companies— was in place, ready for the competition. That structure, of course, was to remain essentially the same until 1982.

Bell and its prospective competitors weren't the only ones getting ready for competition. Consumers in a variety of locations were fed up with poor service and expensive rates. "Where the Bell company enjoyed monopoly privileges," one company historian wrote bluntly, "officials of the company were discourteous and dictatorial, and the service was not satisfactory." In a sense Bell was in a situation similar to that of Eastern Airlines in the New York–Boston–Washington corridor before deregulation (see Chapter Seven). Competitors were itching to get a piece of its lucrative business, and the public apparently was ready for it too.

In the 1890s a number of independent telephone companies strung up their wires and began operation. In some areas, mostly rural, companies like the Michigan Independent Telephone Association set up systems to compete with Bell directly. By 1897 more than 5,000 of these companies had banded together into the National Independent Telephone Association. Bell's response at first was simply to ignore the smaller companies. It couldn't fight them any longer on the basis of patent infringement, and its own business remained good anyway. In the late 1890s, though, the independents were emboldened by their success in the West and began to invade the Northeast. That was the most profitable part of Bell's domain, and the company began to fight back.

Its first tactic was to extend its own service widely. In 1892 it had 240,000 telephones in subscribers' homes and offices; by the end of 1899 the figure topped 800,000. Then too, Bell refused to interconnect with the independents, meaning that subscribers to an independent system couldn't telephone Bell subscribers. And it muscled the competition with price reductions and service improvements, in keeping with good free market practice. As Brooks puts it, "The generally rude and arrogant attitude of Bell officials that had prevailed during monopoly days tended to disappear and be replaced by a more attractive blandness, or even an active desire to please."

Bell's chief weapon, though, was financial. In the 1890s it moved all its assets from American Bell in Boston to the American Telephone and Telegraph Company in New York. That enabled it to get around the capitalization limits imposed by Massachusetts law and thus raise more money. Then it took to buying out the independents, often touching off storms of protest. When a Bell licensee bought the United Telephone Company of Indiana in 1905, for example, the Chicago Corporation Council referred to Bell as a "ruthless, grinding, oppressive monopoly." In fact its maneuvers had not yet come close to making it a monopoly. A count of telephones only two years earlier found Bell with 1,514 telephone exchanges and 1.3 million subscribers. The independents, meanwhile, had 6,150 exchanges and about 2 million subscribers.

Then, in 1907, an alliance of bankers led by J. P. Morgan took control of the company by buying up a substantial fraction of its stock. On May 1 Morgan and his allies installed a new president: Theodore N. Vail. Before, Vail and the company's stockholders hadn't seen eye to eye. Now the new backers were giving him a free rein. He was thus in an ideal position to expound and act upon his philosophy of business—a philosophy, as it turned out, that would guide the system's development for the next several decades.

Theodore N. Vail was a monopolist, at least where telephone service was concerned. "Two exchange systems in the same community," he argued, "cannot be conceived of as a permanency." He believed, however, that monopoly was not just good for the stockholders, it was good for the public as well. "To the public, the Bell System furnishes facilities, in its 'universality' of service and connection, of infinite value to the business world, a service which could not be furnished by dissociated companies. The strength of the Bell System lies in this universality." The telephone company, in other words, was parting company with oil, steel, and other would-be monopolists. Under Vail it would be a public servant as well as a profitable business.

Armed with this ideology and with J. P. Morgan's financial backing, Vail continued buying up competitors—including, in 1909, a controlling interest in Western Union. "The monopoly-bound bandwagon," Brooks observes, "was rolling along." The closer it came to its destination, however, the more likely it seemed to provoke public outcry. In 1913 the attorney general of the United States advised the firm that certain planned acquisitions were in violation of the antitrust laws. That same year the Interstate Commerce Commission began an investigation of Bell. The company was evidently approaching its moment of truth. It would have to give up its efforts to become a monopoly or face the near certainty of antitrust action that might break it up into its component parts.

Faced with this choice, Vail produced a masterstroke of compromise. In a letter from Bell's vice-president Nathan Kingsbury to the Justice Department, the company agreed to divest itself of Western Union, to stop buying out independent companies, and to allow the remaining independents to interconnect with Bell lines. The action, called the Kingsbury Commitment, was a key point in the history of American business, the first major recognition by a giant company that it would have to accommodate itself to the public interest as expressed by government. Ironically it actually hastened the day of the Bell monopoly. Interconnection with the Bell lines effectively subsumed the independents into the system, since every subscriber to an independent company became in effect a Bell customer as well. Gradually many of the remaining companies began to wither away. When in 1921 the Graham Act finally exempted AT&T from the anticompetitive provisions of the Sherman Act, Bell bought up many of the companies that were left. From that day to this it has controlled roughly 85 percent of the nation's phone system, with 1,600 independents dividing up the rest.

Along with his commitment to monopoly as public service, Vail also came to accept the idea of regulation. He astonished the business world by saying in a 1915 speech that he had no objection to regulation, "provided it is independent, intelligent, considerate, thorough, and just." "Society has never allowed that which is necessary to existence to be controlled by private interest," he argued. Regulatory bodies should act as juries, "protecting the individual member of the public against corporate aggression or extortion, and the corporate member of the community against public extortion and aggression." They could also, he conceded, suppress "certain evils that have been engrained in our commercial practices."

Thus Vail not only set AT&T against the prevailing ideology of laissez faire and free competition, he also set out a theory of the proper relationship between business and government. That theory is very close to that which prevails today. Years before Coolidge's dictum as to the business of America, Vail was arguing that a corporation is a member of the community, with the power to serve or abuse it—and that, as Brooks puts it, "maximum private profit was not necessarily the primary objective of private enterprise." His views, though hardly characteristic of business leaders, would be echoed in different settings by a few others, such as General Electric's Owen D. Young. These leaders, in effect, foreshadowed the consensus as to the role of business that would emerge in the post–New Deal era.

AT&T TRAVAILS, however, continued. A federal antitrust suit filed in 1949 sought to split off Western Electric from the parent company. That suit perked on for several years; finally in 1956 it was settled by a consent decree. AT&T, said the decree, could keep Western Electric. But Western Electric could make only telephone equipment and the Bell System could not engage in any electronics or communications business *except* telephone service and work for the U.S. government. It could keep its monopoly, but it couldn't stray beyond it.

This decree might have worked indefinitely but for two developments. One was that court decisions kept whittling away at Bell's monopoly. In the 1960s, for example, a small businessman named Tom Carter invented a device called the Carterfone, an instrument designed to connect a mobile radio with a telephone. AT&T went to court to prevent him from selling it. Eventually the case wound up before the Federal Communications Commission, which—in a landmark decision—ruled for Carter. That decision effectively stripped AT&T of its monopoly over telephone equipment and accessories and gave rise to what has become known as the competitive interconnect industry. By the late 1970s whole offices were being outfitted with complex key telephone systems manufactured and installed by Bell's competitors and connected into Bell's lines.

At the same time, a host of companies began to offer competitive long-distance telephone service. The leader in this field was MCI Telecommunications Corporation, which first gained the right to tie into the AT&T system. Subscribers who signed up with MCI got a special code to dial along with their long-distance calls; dialing the code hooked them into MCI's extensive microwave relay system, which forwarded their call to its destination. In 1982 the company counted some 850,000 subscribers in 200 different cities, and claimed to save these customers anywhere from 15 to 50 percent on their phone bills. Other companies began to offer a similar service, among them ITT and Sprint, the latter a venture owned by the Southern Pacific Company. Togther the independents in 1982 shared about 3 percent of the long-distance market—not much by their lights but 3 percentage points more than Bell was accustomed to.

As Bell was retreating on these fronts, though, it was advancing on another. In the 1970s the dazzling new field of computerized communications seemed likely to mushroom into a $100 billion

market. The FCC allowed Bell to set up an unregu-
lated subsidiary to compete in this field, a move
that provoked howls of protest from Bell's would-be
competitors. As H.G.W. Biddle, a Washington lawyer who represented some of these competitors, explained their viewpoint: "We don't feel AT&T should
own the highways as well as manufacture the trucks
and control the loading docks and all the other
things that make it possible for others to ship over
the highway system." From its own point of view,
however, AT&T was ideally suited to enter the field.
Not only did it have direct access to the telephone
system, it also had virtually unmatched expertise in
electronics. The only thing that worried it was the
antitrust threat.

And in fact the Justice Department had filed yet
another antitrust suit against AT&T in 1974. This
suit proposed to dismember the system entirely on
the grounds that certain of its actions had violated
part of the Sherman Act. In answering the suit,
AT&T counsel George Saunders argued that antitrust theory was obsolete in an era of government
regulation. The Bell System, he pointed out, was
extensively regulated on the state level, and the
1956 consent decree had boxed the company in
completely, keeping it out of markets that did not
fall within its circumscribed area. Saunders's argument was an attempt to settle once and for all the
tangled questions of regulation, competition, and
monopoly. But the new competition on the one
hand and the possibility of new markets on the
other made his argument obsolete. When the suit
was settled, Bell found itself on brand-new turf.

The settlement came in 1982, and it was a bombshell. According to its terms, AT&T would divest itself of its 22 regional operating companies. It would keep Bell Labs and Western Electric, and it would be essentially free to compete in the new field of computer-related communications. "There comes a time, and this was it," said AT&T chairman Charles L. Brown after the settlement was announced. "We had to make some bold move to cut through the tangle" of court, congressional, and regulatory restraints.

At first the settlement seemed to some like a defeat for Bell. But slowly its advantages to the company became apparent. The operating companies, for example, are the weak link in the company's chain of profits. Though they enjoy a guaranteed rate of return, they are the most closely regulated, the slowest growing, and the most capital intensive part of the industry. The parent company got rid of those but kept its long-distance service, Bell Labs, and Western Electric, all highly profitable. It would now be able to move aggressively into the computer communications field without fear of government intervention. Richard Wiley, a former FCC chairman, called AT&T's agreement "a brilliant masterstroke. They gave away the future railroads of this industry, kept the moneymakers they already had, and won the right to go after everything else on the high-revenue side." And as the *Boston Globe* financial writer Ron Rosenberg observed, "While AT&T takes on competitors in the open environment, [the] operating companies will be forced to continue going hat-in-hand to the regulatory authorities for more money."

The AT&T settlement did not please everyone. A Harris poll sponsored by the company after the settlement indicated that the public feared the breakup would lead to higher telephone rates. The fear, presumably, was that local operating companies would be financially weak when set adrift by Bell. At the same time, however, 83 percent supported the settlement "if it allows AT&T to compete freely and fully with any competitors in developing new computerized uses of the telephone system." In Congress, Rep. Timothy Wirth (D-Colo.) filed a bill designed to overrule the consent decree. In its place the bill mandated divestiture of long-distance service as well as the operating companies and increased the FCC's powers over Bell's operation. "The bill purports to protect the interests of local telephone users and of the Bell operating companies that are to be divested," wrote AT&T chairman Brown in an angry letter to shareholders, urging them to oppose the bill. "But its principal supporters . . . are competitors—including foreign competitors—whose main objective appears to be to protect their own interests by preventing us from competing in markets that we are well-equipped to serve."

The fallout from the 1982 settlement seemed likely to continue for some time. One of its provisions was to give competitors like MCI the same access as AT&T to local telephone networks, and the independents were looking hungrily at this opportunity. "It should give us much bigger markets, a much higher-quality service, and much more convenience in using our service," MCI's president, V. Orville Wright, told a reporter. "Therefore, we should be able to get considerably more market share." To date, for example, MCI had been limited to connecting with the Bell system's so-called Touch-Tone phones, which were in use in only 40 percent of the market.

Equal access would ensure the firm connections with rotary-dial phones and might make it possible for its customers to dial only eleven digits for a long-distance call instead of the twenty previously required.

In the meantime Bell would gear itself up for full-scale competition, not only in phone service but in computerized communications and other data-transfer applications. The ultimate result, it seemed, would not harken back to the days when small towns sometimes had two separate phone systems and two exchanges. But it would, in all likelihood, involve a degree of competition that hadn't been seen since the 1890s.

THE HISTORY of the Bell System reflects a peculiarly American attitude toward business in one important way. For all its travails, Bell has remained a company owned and controlled by its stockholders and their elected board of directors. As such it is unusual in the Western world. Most telephone systems in Europe, for instance, are owned and operated by the government, often in conjunction with the postal system. In this, of course, the telephone system is not unique. Many European governments also run the railroads, an airline, and diverse enterprises ranging from steel mills and oil companies to investment banks. America, historically, has had little truck with government-run enterprises of this sort.

Should a big company like AT&T be nationalized? A European socialist—or an American one, for that matter—would answer that a government-run company is better able to serve the public than a privately owned one. The nationalized enterprise, so the argument runs, puts service ahead of profits. Business that is needed by society but that isn't always profitable—serving sparsely populated areas, for example—doesn't get put on the back burner. The fact that company directors and managers are public officials means that they will take social goals as well as institutional objectives into account, and any profits they may generate will flow to the national treasury rather than the pockets of wealthy shareholders.

Free enterprisers, of course, have answers to all these arguments. Profits, they say, can be realized only when the public is served. If society has objectives that private enterprise does not meet—a clean environment, for instance, or equal employment opportunity—the proper redress is a law or regulation setting the framework in which all firms must operate. To nationalize a company is not only to risk inefficiency and "politicization" of the concern but to take property that is lawfully owned by citizens and entrust it to the dubious hands of government.

Advocates of both points of view have favorite examples to point to. Free enterprisers invariably hold up the Postal Service as a model of sloth and corruption. They also note—correctly—that the Bell System is universally acknowledged as the best telephone system in the world. Socialists and other advocates of nationalization point to the alleged abuses of private economic power by oil companies and other giant concerns and to the generally honest and efficient operation of many European state-run enterprises. Closer to home they also note that some small, government-owned enterprises like municipal electric companies frequently offer better service at cheaper rates than their investor-owned counterparts.

To some extent the debate turns on different conceptions of a business's purpose, a topic taken up in the epilogue to this book. To some extent it depends on how one weighs the evidence—and whether, for instance, it seems possible for Americans, who are born and bred to free enterprise, to adopt European models. Most of all, of course, it turns on politics and pragmatism. When a company works as well as AT&T has in the recent past, and when the public interest has been well provided for through regulation, few Americans would advocate nationalization. When companies seem to be failing (like the railroads) or seem to be abusing their enormous economic power (like the oil companies), nationalization may look attractive.

It would be surprising, though, if nationalization ever caught on in America to the same extent it has in Western Europe. The tradition of free enterprise in the United States runs deep, and the forces that would oppose any such move are strong. Most likely, business and government will continue to jockey for position, sometimes cooperating and sometimes coming into conflict. Regulation and competition will continue to play an important role, as will laws that set limits on the proper scope and purview of private enterprise.

Americans' attitudes toward business, after all, are neither adoring (as they once were) nor scornful. Most Americans believe that business should be restricted or rewarded by one measure alone—how well it does its job.

Epilogue

NEARLY TWENTY YEARS AGO the sociologist Andrew Hacker invented a provocative parable illustrating a paradox of corporate power. The parable, which appeared in a book called *The Corporation Take-Over*, told the story of a fictitious concern called American Electric.

By 1972 Hacker said (his dates have an amusing ring from our vantage point), American Electric had completed its last stages of automation. Employees were no longer needed: "Raw materials left on the loading platform were automatically transferred from machine to machine, and the finished products were deposited at the other end of the factory ready for shipment." All the company's other functions—marketing, purchasing, general management, and so on—"could be handled by ten directors with the occasional help of outside consultants and contractors."

Several years before, the company's pension fund had invested heavily in AE stock, eventually buying up all the outstanding shares. As employees retired or were forced out by automation, the fund began selling these shares to provide for pensions. It sold them not to other investors but to AE itself, which thus provided the money for pensions out of current income. Soon, as the last employee died and the fund went out of business, AE was the sole owner of its shares.

In 1982, Hacker continues, "the ten directors decided that AE would be well served by the passage of legislation restricting the imports of certain electrical equipment." They engaged a public relations firm and mounted a massive advertising campaign on the issue, spending several million dollars. "Within months the public began to hear about the dire consequences that would follow the importation of alien generators. National security, national prosperity, and the nation's way of life were threatened. . . . At least fifty citizens' committees 'spontaneously' arose to favor the legislation, and over two hundred existing groups passed resolutions of support. Lectures were given to women's clubs, and films were shown in high schools. By the end of the year—an election year—public sentiment had been aroused and hardly a Congressman was unaware of the popular ferment."

Prodded by such efforts, the bill AE sought passed handily and was signed by the president. AE's profits the next year went up substantially. "A group of senators, however, was curious about what had been going on, and they decided to investigate AE's foray into the political arena." Since the company had done nothing illegal, one of the directors was glad to testify. After recounting the firm's activities, he concluded, "It was our view that they were dictated by the company's best interests."

That phrase puzzled the senator who happened to be asking the questions. Who, he wondered, was the company? The stockholders? No; the director explained that the firm no longer had any stockholders. The workers? No again, there were no employees. The senator got angry. "Then so far as I can see," he said, "all of this political pressure that you applied was really in the interests of yourself and your nine fellow directors. You spent almost six million dollars of this company's money pursuing your personal predilections."

The director was outraged at this suggestion. He pointed out to the senator that all ten directors got only an annual salary—a handsome one, to be sure, but not one that depended on the firm's profit level. They conscientiously took no bonuses or incentive pay. As private citizens, moreover, at least eight of the ten directors opposed the legislation, thinking it against the national interest. Their role, however, was not to wish their own preferences on the company; it was to do what they thought best for the firm. "We are just doing the job for which we were hired," the director concluded—"to look out for the company's interests."

THIS BOOK has explored the elements of enterprise. Early chapters reviewed the fundamentals: entrepreneurship, the marketplace, risk. Later ones examined the tasks a business must accomplish if it is to succeed and what happens if it fails. The last chapter traced the history of business's changing role in society, as illustrated by the unique story of the Bell System.

Most of the book, concerned as it is with business strategies, necessarily takes for granted the answer to a fundamental question. What is the purpose of a business? What should be the objectives of enterprise? These issues cropped up in the last chapter—no discussion of a company as large and as pervasive as AT&T could ignore them—but in my view they merit further reflection. Though they seem like the sort of topics best left to philosophers and other academicians, they are not. On the contrary, our views as to business's proper function affect our views on some of today's most pressing political issues: free trade, environmental protection, unemployment. The question of corporate purpose is thus as timely as it is vexing.

The simplest and most frequent answer to the question is one word: profit. A business's job is to make money. This view has a certain elegance to it, harking as it does back to Adam Smith. It also has the virtue of undeniability. If a business doesn't make money, it can't survive, and then whatever else it may wish to accomplish won't be done either.

But is profit a sufficient as well as a necessary objective of a business enterprise? Profit for whom and to what end? As Hacker's parable suggests, the "corporate interest" in profit can be quite abstract, even antithetical to a variety of real human interests. The successful effort of "American Electric" to ban foreign competition restricted the supply of electrical equipment, thus keeping prices high and forcing consumers to depend on existing suppliers. And the parable, while farfetched, is not wholly without parallel in the real world. A big corporation's shareholders, after all, are typically a faceless lot, buying into companies or selling out of them as the market dictates. Doubtless any corporation's management has an obligation to protect, and in the long run to enhance, these shareholders' investment. But that profit should be the firm's only objective—and that it should seek profit to the exclusion of everything else—is no longer a proposition that commands much support.

The challenge to the notion that a business should pursue profits pure and simple has come from at least four different quarters, each one reflecting a different set of concerns.

From a business point of view, first, numerous economists and management specialists have argued that a corporation's first priority is not and should not be short-term profit. Rather it should be growth. Recall briefly Loy Weston's remark about the Japanese tolerance for "eight down quarters," meaning two years of marginal profitability. The Japanese, he said, were willing to tolerate such a period, provided the company was expanding its market share and thus growing rapidly. U.S. stock analysts, however, would "sell your stock tomorrow." Weston is not alone in his concern. A variety of analysts have charged that American managers' fixation on short-term profitability leads them to forgo long-term productivity-enhancing investments. Managers, these critics charge, spend too much time worrying about this year's bottom line. Their superiors are too quick to judge the managers' performance by this criterion alone.

The difference between the long-term, growth-oriented perspective and a short-term profit objective is quite real. When a business is owned by one person—Tom Gentry, say, or Marvin Kroeger—the owner can singlehandedly balance his priorities, taking what he chooses out of the business now and plowing in what he chooses in expectation of future growth. When an enterprise is owned by absentee stockholders, however, management is making a decision for them. Those who for whatever reason are planning to hold their stock only a short time are likely to be hurt financially by managers pursuing long-term goals. Without the long-term perspective, though, it is hard to see how the U.S. economy can remain competitive in the world economy, particularly vis-à-vis the Japanese. Does a corporation have an interest in maintaining this competitiveness over the long haul? Managers can move on to other jobs, and shareholders can sell out, but we can't dismantle the whole economy.

From labor's perspective, an enterprise has a second set of objectives. It exists to provide jobs. Moreover, it should pay its employees a fair wage, and it should provide them with safe, decent working conditions. As Chapter Eight revealed, these issues have been bones of contention throughout American business history, with improvements coming only after a good deal of protest and turmoil. In some ways, though, we have not come as far as the Japanese or some European countries. Since one of a Japanese company's purposes is assumed to be the provision of secure employment for its workers, the issue of jobs is that much less contentious. Western European firms too are more sensitive to their role as employment providers, particularly those that depend on government support. Airbus Industrie, for example, refuses to add many new workers whenever it has a big order because it will have to lay them off when the order is completed. It thus operates with a bigger backlog than an American firm like Boeing, which expands and contracts more easily with market conditions.

The corporation's role in providing employment comes to the fore precisely when that role is threatened. Lockheed and Chrysler won their government bailouts mainly because of the jobs that would be lost if the two giant corporations went under. John Z. DeLorean got as much help as he did from the British government because of the jobs he promised to create and maintain. In recent years failing companies have sometimes been bought up by their employees, precisely for the purpose of saving jobs. The Hyatt Clark Company in New Jersey, for instance—a General Motors subsidiary—was bought out by its employees when GM threatened to shut it down. Similar "worker takeovers" have occurred elsewhere.

From the consumer's point of view, the corporation's purpose is to provide goods and services that are safe, useful, well made, and reasonably priced. In theory the market ensures that firms will pursue this objective: if they don't pay attention to consumers' wants, they won't be able to sell their wares. The reality, of course, is not quite so simple. Most products of an industrial society are complex. Consumers aren't always able to judge the merits of a product. They are not always able to choose freely between competing products. And defects may not show up till years after purchase. Asbestos-based building materials, for instance, have been thought in some instances to cause asbestos-related respiratory diseases. But the diseases do not develop for twenty years after exposure to asbestos, and the exposure itself may have been involuntary. Few consumers ask what the walls are made of when they enter a public building or even when they buy a house.

The "consumer revolution" pioneered by Ralph Nader and symbolized by agencies like the Consumer Product Safety Commission has done much to ensure that companies really will take consumer needs into account. The recent growth in product-liability and other consumer-related lawsuits has had the same effect. So, finally, have changes in the marketplace itself. All three factors can be seen at work in the airline business, for example. For many years the airlines routinely followed a practice of overbooking flights, with the well-justified expectation that not all passengers who made reservations would actually show up for the flight. If too many did show up, a few were simply "bumped" off the flight on to the next available plane—which might have been the next day. Now, thanks to a lawsuit started by Nader himself, passengers who are bumped must be given all-expenses-paid transportation to their destination as quickly as possible. If accommodations are required, the airline must pay. Ironically the law might not have to enforce these regulations in the new age of airline competition. An advertised "no-bumping" policy might give New York Air or any other upstart the competitive edge it needs to take on giants like Eastern.

Finally, from the surrounding community's point of view, companies have an obligation to be good citizens and good neighbors. This might mean not only that they provide employment and useful goods or services but also that they conduct their business in such a way as to improve the quality of life in their communities. This objective has not always been avidly pursued by businesses. Factories frequently pollute the air with smoke and the rivers with waste, fight zoning restrictions, oppose tax increases, and ignore community activities. But regulations have ended or mitigated many such practices, and corporate "good-neighbor" policies have in some places replaced the old "business is business" attitude. The conflicts, to be sure, have not disappeared. But it is much more widely accepted than it used to be that companies have an obligation to both their neighbors and the rest of us.

NONE OF THESE GOALS—long-term growth, employment, responsibility to consumers and the community—is inconsistent with making a good profit. Some would argue that a company pursuing all of them stands the best long-term chance of success. Despite both these statements, however, objectives frequently conflict in the here and now. Entrepreneurs and managers, who must operate from day to day, somehow have to balance a set of diverse objectives. Nor are these objectives abstract. On the contrary, shareholders, workers, consumer groups, government agencies, and local officials are seldom loath to express their opinions as to what companies should and should not do. If an enterprise can satisfy most of those who make demands on it, and if it can at the same time make money, it is probably attaining a broad range of goals.

In the past the split between profit and other goals was often reflected in the careers of individual entrepreneurs. John D. Rockefeller's name was once synonymous with ruthless wheeling and dealing. Andrew Carnegie was a dour Scot with a reputation for penny pinching and union busting. Henry Ford was known as a hard man to work for. Yet today the names of all three men grace major foundations known worldwide for their philanthropic activities. The irony in all this is that it was precisely the great capitalists' wealth that made it possible for them and their descendants to become philanthropists. Similarly it is precisely the companies that are most successful that are also most widely known for their extracurricular activities. Xerox, Polaroid, and Levi Strauss all have reputations for progressive social policies within the firm and charitable endeavors outside of it. And all, of course, have for most of the last twenty years been highly profitable. Companies that are struggling for existence, or that are faced with intense competitive pressures, can afford neither the time nor the money to plan, pay for, and carry out good works.

A similar irony is reflected in the issue of company size. Americans have always been ambivalent toward big business: respecting its contribution on the one hand, they have resented its power on the other. Certainly there is little doubt that many big firms are prone to an arrogance of power and that many are bureaucratic monstrosities, as prone as any government agency to the sclerosis and insensitivity of large organizations. Yet it is the big firms, for the most part, that pay their workers above-average wages; that have pioneered in providing health insurance, pension plans, and other benefits; and that finance nonprofit institutions ranging from universities to public television stations. An economy of small, fiercely competitive companies, satisfying though it might be from a free marketeer's perspective, would not be so easily able to pursue objectives other than a favorable showing on this year's bottom line.

BECAUSE ENTERPRISES are made up of people and must live in society—because they are different from the fictitious company of Andrew Hacker's parable—they must somehow pursue a variety of objectives and serve a variety of needs. The conventional economic notion of the marketplace, in short, may be too narrow. Companies do, of course, have to operate at a profit. But they also have to meet the needs of workers, consumers, and the community, and they have somehow to balance long-term concerns with short-term ones.

The great strength of the Japanese economy may lie precisely here—in the Japanese corporation's ability to command widespread support and assistance because it serves so many people's needs so well. American firms have frequently taken a go-it-alone approach, assuming their job was to make money and someone else's job was to look out for everything else. In the 1980s, with energy scarce and international competition acute, this approach may no longer work. What may be needed instead is a broader conception of business's purpose, one that can engage support from all segments of society.

This will not make the job of the businessman or businesswoman any easier. He or she will still have to accomplish all the tasks described in this book and do so in a way that satisfies the firm's customers, rewards its workers, and serves its community. Yet if the manager's job isn't easier, it may be more challenging and ultimately more satisfying. Enterprise, after all, is only as good as the people who make it go. A broad conception of the purpose of business should attract people who, even as they want to make a living, also want to make living worthwhile, for others as well as for themselves.

INDEX

Business Guides from MENTOR and SIGNET

(0451)

☐ **UNDERSTANDING FINANCIAL STATEMENTS by John N. Myer.** Here at last is a book that makes financial statements truly easy to understand whether you are an executive or investor interested in profits, or a student of business administration. No previous knowledge of accounting is necessary. (620518—$2.50)

☐ **AN ACCOUNTING PRIMER by Elwin W. Midgett.** The ABC's of accounting for the non-accountant. Here is a lean, readable guide, free of complex technical language, which teaches you how to apply the practices and principles of accounting to your business and your personal finances. A special section includes a dictionary of definitions which explores in detail the various subdivisions in the field of accounting. (621530—$2.50)

☐ **DYNAMIC INVESTING: The System for Automatic Profits— No Matter Which Way the Market Goes by Jerome Tuccille.** Revised and updated edition reflecting the new tax laws. "The new set of rules the investor needs to play by . . . A technically sound approach to investment in the '80s."—Grace W. Weinstein, in *Good Housekeeping* (116259—$2.50)*

☐ **THE SMART INVESTOR'S GUIDE TO THE MONEY MARKET by Paul Sarnoff.** A leading broker tells you how to outfox inflation and put your money to work for you as never before! (111184—$3.50)

☐ **TAX SHELTERS by Robert and Carol Tannenhauser.** In simple, concise language, a top lawyer explains the latest legislation and rulings as you learn what tax shelters exist, how they work, how to evaluate the advantages and risks, and how they can best benefit you. Including cash-flow charts that plot savings through 1989, and a glossary that turns technical terms and IRS-ese into plain English. (125436—$3.95)

*Prices slightly higher in Canada
